Texas Assessment Preparation

Grade 7

HOLT McDOUGAL

Literature

Texas

TEXAS WRITE SOURCE

HOUGHTON MIFFLIN HARCOURT

Printed in the U.S.A.

ISBN 978-0-547-74910-5

4 5 6 7 8 9 10 0982 20 19 18 17 16 15 14 13 12

4500365710 A B C D E F G

Contents

Written Composition

Revising and Editing

PART II: *TEXAS WRITE SOURCE* ASSESSMENTS

How to Use This Book

Texas Assessment Preparation contains instruction that will help you develop the reading and writing skills tested on the State of Texas Assessments of Academic Readiness (STAAR). In addition, this book includes tests that accompany the Houghton Mifflin Harcourt *Texas Write Source* program.

PART I: PREPARING FOR TEXAS ASSESSMENTS

Part I of the book will help you develop skills assessed on the STAAR test. It consists of two basic types of instruction:

- **Guided instruction** materials offer annotations, citations from the Texas Essential Knowledge and Skills (TEKS), and answer explanations, plus models and rubrics for written composition. Annotations highlight the key skills you will need to apply. Sample questions, answer explanations, models, and rubrics help you analyze each question or prompt and its correct response.
- **Practice** materials give you the opportunity to apply what you have learned to assessments like those you will be taking near the end of your school year.

Part I is divided into the following sections:

Reading

The readings from a variety of genres give you opportunities to practice the essential reading skills outlined in the TEKS for your grade. Initially, as you read the Guided Reading passages, annotations and shading offer detailed explanations that draw attention to specific TEKS-based skills. After you have finished reading, you can review and hone test-taking skills by analyzing sample multiple-choice items, their answers, and answer explanations. Following guided instruction, you will independently practice essential reading and assessment skills. For these Reading Practice lessons, you will read selections and answer multiple-choice items crafted to cover a range of appropriate TEKS and reading comprehension skills.

One feature of the Reading Practice materials in this book is a column headed "**My notes about what I am reading.**" You can improve your comprehension skills by using this column to monitor your reading abilities.

As you read the Reading Practice selections, take advantage of the "My notes about what I am reading" column by using it to make notes about the following topics:

- Key ideas or events
- Initial or overall impressions of characters, situations, or topics, including how each is like someone or something familiar to you
- Guesses at the meaning of any unfamiliar words or phrases
- Questions or points of confusion
- Ideas about why the author wrote the selection
- Comments about what you would like to know more about
- Your own ideas about the meaning of ideas or events or how they might apply to the real world

In addition, you may want to mark the selection text itself. You can, for example, circle, underscore, or highlight words or phrases that seem important or about which you have questions.

Written Composition

This section provides you with model essay prompts, sample essays, and scoring rubrics. These resources give you opportunities to practice the writing process for genres that will be tested. First, annotations will guide you as you analyze sample prompts and 2- and 4-point model responses. Then, you will practice your writing skills independently by responding to similar TEKS-aligned prompts.

Revising and Editing

In the multiple-choice format of this section, you will practice TEKS-based revising and editing skills. First, you will receive guided instruction in revising or editing. You will read sample essays, review assessment items, and analyze answer explanations. Then, you will work on independent practice, in which you identify editing or revising issues in sample essays and answer multiple-choice items crafted to cover a range of appropriate revising or editing TEKS.

PART II: *TEXAS WRITE SOURCE* ASSESSMENTS

The *Texas Write Source* assessments are a set of four tests designed to help you measure your progress in *Texas Write Source.*

- The **Pretest** should be completed at the beginning of the school year. It can help you measure your level of writing experience and knowledge and what your teacher might need to emphasize in your instruction. The **Pretest** also provides a baseline for measuring your progress from the beginning of the year to the end.
- **Progress Test 1** and **Progress Test 2** should be completed at regular intervals during the year. These tests can help you and your teacher monitor your progress as the school year proceeds.
- The **Post-test** should be completed at the end of the year to show how much progress you have made.

Each test has three parts. ***Part 1: Basic Elements of Writing*** and ***Part 2: Proofreading and Editing*** comprise a total of 30 multiple-choice questions. You will choose the best answer to each question. ***Part 3: Writing*** provides a writing prompt. You will respond by writing a composition.

NOTE: Every effort has been made to incorporate the latest information available about STAAR at the time of publication.

Part I

Preparing for Texas Assessments

Guided Reading

Reading Literary Text: Fiction

In this part of the book, you will read a short story with instruction about the elements of fiction. Following the selection are sample questions and answers about the story. The purpose of this section is to show you how to understand and analyze fiction.

To begin, review the TEKS that relate to fictional texts:

FICTION TEKS	WHAT IT MEANS TO YOU
(6) Comprehension of Literary Text/Fiction Students understand, make inferences and draw conclusions about the structure and elements of fiction and provide evidence from text to support their understanding. Students are expected to:	
(A) explain the influence of setting on plot development;	You will discuss how the time and place in which a story is set affect the way the story develops.
(B) analyze the development of the plot through the internal and external responses of the characters, including their motivations and conflicts; and	You will analyze plot development and how a character's motives and conflicts (both within and outside of themselves) affect the way the story develops.
(C) analyze different forms of point of view, including first-person, third-person omniscient, and third-person limited.	You will analyze the differences between the different points of view from which a story is told.

The selection that follows provides instruction in the fiction TEKS as well as other TEKS. It also covers reading comprehension skills, such as making inferences and reflecting on your understanding of text.

As you read the story "The Fun They Had," notice how the author uses the literary elements of plot, character development, and point of view. The annotations in the margins will guide you as you read.

Name ______________________ Date ______________

Guided Reading

Read this selection. Then answer the questions that follow.

The Fun They Had

by Isaac Asimov

The following story takes place in the future. However, it was written in 1951, when computers were huge machines that were kept in refrigerated buildings. These computers were very different from the small, powerful personal computers that we use today.

1 Margie even wrote about it that night in her diary. On the page headed May 17, 2155, she wrote, "Today Tommy found a real book!"

2 It was a very old book. Margie's grandfather once said that when he was a little boy, *his* grandfather told him that there was a time when all stories were printed on paper.

3 They turned the pages, which were yellow and crinkly, and it was awfully funny to read words that stood still instead of moving the way they were supposed to—on a screen, you know. And then, when they turned back to the page before, it had the same words on it that it had when they read it the first time.

4 "Gee," said Tommy, "what a waste. When you're through with the book, you just throw it away, I guess. Our television screen must have had a million books on it and it's good for plenty more. I wouldn't throw *it* away."

5 "Same with mine," said Margie. She was eleven and hadn't seen as many telebooks as Tommy had. He was thirteen.

6 She said, "Where did you find it?"

7 "In my house." He pointed without looking, because he was busy reading. "In the attic."

8 "What's it about?"

9 "School."

SETTING
The author draws you into the story with specific details about when the story takes place. These details are also a clue to how important the setting will be to the plot of the story.

TEKS 6A

CONTEXT CLUES
If you don't know the word *telebooks* in paragraph 5, look for context clues in the surrounding text. From the clue "Our television screen must have had a million books on it," you can guess that a *telebook* is a book that can be read on a television screen.

TEKS 2B

GO ON

Name ________________________________ Date ______________

10 Margie was scornful. "School? What's there to write about school? I hate school." Margie always hated school, but now she hated it more than ever. The mechanical teacher had been giving her test after test in geography, and she had been doing worse and worse until her mother had shaken her head sorrowfully and sent for the county inspector.

11 He was a round little man with a red face and a whole box of tools with dials and wires. He smiled at her and gave her an apple, then took the teacher apart. Margie had hoped he wouldn't know how to put it together again, but he knew how all right, and after an hour or so, there it was again, large and ugly, with a big screen on which all the lessons were shown and the questions were asked. That wasn't so bad. The part she hated most was the slot where she had to put homework and test papers. She always had to write them out in a punch code[1] they made her learn when she was six years old, and the mechanical teacher calculated the mark in no time.

12 The inspector had smiled after he was finished and patted her head. He said to her mother, "It's not the little girl's fault, Mrs. Jones. I think the geography sector was geared a little too quick. Those things happen sometimes. I've slowed it up to an average ten-year level. Actually, the overall pattern of her progress is quite satisfactory." And he patted Margie's head again.

13 Margie was disappointed. She had been hoping they would take the teacher away altogether. They had once taken Tommy's teacher away for nearly a month because the history sector had blanked out completely.

14 So she said to Tommy, "Why would anyone write about school?"

15 Tommy looked at her with very superior eyes. "Because it's not our kind of school, stupid. This is the old kind of school that they had hundreds and hundreds of years ago." He added loftily, pronouncing the word carefully, "*Centuries ago.*"

16 Margie was hurt. "Well, I don't know what kind of school they had all that time ago." She read the book over his shoulder for a while, then said, "Anyway, they had a teacher."

17 "Sure they had a teacher, but it wasn't a regular teacher. It was a man."

POINT OF VIEW
In literature, a narrator tells the story. The author's choice of narrator is referred to as point of view. The point of view in this selection is called third-person limited because the narrator is someone outside the story and is describing the thoughts and feelings of only one character—Margie.

TEKS 6C

CHARACTER MOTIVATION
A character's motivation is the reason he or she acts a certain way. A character's motivation can affect the plot of a story. In paragraph 11, you learn Margie's motivation for not wanting the inspector to fix the mechanical teacher.

TEKS 6B

CONTEXT CLUES
If you don't know the word *geared* in paragraph 12, look for context clues in words and phrases near it. The phrases "a little too quick" and "I've slowed it up" can help you figure out that *geared* means "adjusted."

TEKS 2B

1. **punch code:** an old-fashioned way of storing computer data in which holes are punched in paper.

GO ON

Name ______________________________ Date ______________

18 "A man? How could a man be a teacher?"

19 "Well, he just told the boys and girls things and gave them homework and asked them questions."

20 "A man isn't smart enough."

21 "Sure he is. My father knows as much as my teacher."

22 "He can't. A man can't know as much as a teacher."

23 "He knows almost as much I betcha."[2]

24 Margie wasn't prepared to dispute that. She said, "I wouldn't want a strange man in my house to teach me."

25 Tommy screamed with laughter. "You don't know much, Margie. The teachers didn't live in the house. They had a special building and all the kids went there."

26 "And all the kids learned the same thing?"

27 "Sure, if they were the same age."

28 "But my mother says a teacher has to be adjusted to fit the mind of each boy and girl it teaches and that each kid has to be taught differently."

29 "Just the same, they didn't do it that way then. If you don't like it, you don't have to read the book."

30 "I didn't say I didn't like it," Margie said quickly. She wanted to read about those funny schools.

31 They weren't even half finished when Margie's mother called, "Margie! School!"

32 Margie looked up. "Not yet, Mamma."

33 "Now," said Mrs. Jones. "And it's probably time for Tommy, too."

34 Margie said to Tommy, "Can I read the book some more with you after school?"

35 "Maybe," he said, nonchalantly.[3] He walked away whistling, the dusty old book tucked beneath his arm.

EXTERNAL CONFLICT
In most stories, the plot centers on conflict, the struggle between opposing forces. An external conflict is a struggle between a character and an outside force. This force could be another character. In paragraphs 15 and 16, Margie is having a conflict with Tommy.

TEKS 6B

INTERNAL CONFLICT
An internal conflict is a conflict that takes place within a character. In paragraphs 22–28, Margie's idea of a teacher is in conflict with the information she is getting from Tommy.

TEKS 6B

2. **I betcha:** slang for "I bet you."
3. **nonchalantly:** in a casual way.

GO ON

Name ______________________________ Date ______________

36 Margie went into the schoolroom. It was right next to her bedroom, and the mechanical teacher was on and waiting for her. It was always on at the same time every day except Saturday and Sunday, because her mother said little girls learned better if they learned at regular hours.

37 The screen was lit up, and it said: "Today's arithmetic lesson is on the addition of proper fractions. Please insert yesterday's homework in the proper slot."

38 Margie did so with a sigh. She was thinking about the old schools they had when her grandfather's grandfather was a little boy. All the kids from the whole neighborhood came, laughing and shouting in the schoolyard, sitting together in the schoolroom, going home together at the end of the day. They learned the same things so they could help one another on the homework and talk about it.

39 And the teachers were people. . . .

40 The mechanical teacher was flashing on the screen: "When we add the fractions 1/2 and 1/4 . . ."

41 Margie was thinking about how the kids must have loved it in the old days. She was thinking about the fun they had.

MAKING INFERENCES
As a reader, you must figure out what the author is not telling you directly. You can fill in these gaps by combining details from the text with your own knowledge and experiences. In paragraphs 38 and 39, Margie thinks about how different school was hundreds of years ago. From this information you can infer her feelings about her own schoolroom and the schools of long ago.

Fig. 19D

GO ON

Name ______________________ Date ______________

Use "The Fun They Had" (pp. 5–8) to answer questions 1–6.

1 The story's point of view helps the reader understand why —

A Tommy tells Margie about a book he found

B Margie's mother was worried about Margie's homework

C Margie would like to have a person as a teacher

D the inspector gave Margie an apple

EXPLANATION: This story is told from a third-person limited point of view. The narrator is an observer who comments on the actions and thoughts of only one character in the story. **C** is correct because the narrator reveals only Margie's thoughts. Margie hates her mechanical teacher and thinks the idea of a real person as a teacher is appealing.

- **A** is incorrect because the narrator does not reveal Tommy's thoughts.
- **B** is incorrect because the narrator does not reveal the mother's thoughts.
- **D** is incorrect because the narrator does not reveal the inspector's thoughts.

TEKS 6C

2 Read the following dictionary entry.

> **sector** \sĕk′ tər\ *n.* **1.** part of a circle **2.** a measuring instrument with two arms hinged together **3.** a certain military area or zone **4.** a part, section, or division of something

What is the definition of sector as it is used in paragraph 12?

F Definition 1

G Definition 2

H Definition 3

J Definition 4

EXPLANATION: The story mentions a geography sector inside one mechanical teacher and a history sector inside another mechanical teacher. From the context of the story, you can tell that a sector is part of the mechanical teacher. **J** is correct.

- **F** is incorrect because the mechanical teacher is not a circle.
- **G** is incorrect. Although the mechanical teacher grades papers, it is not a measuring device with two arms hinged together.
- **H** is incorrect because the mechanical teacher does not contain a military area or zone.

TEKS 2B

GO ON

Name ______________________________ Date ______________

3 Which of the following best describes the importance of the setting to the plot of the story?

A The reader knows that Margie wrote in her diary.

B The reader learns how schools are different in 2155.

C The reader knows that the story starts on May 17, 2155.

D The reader knows what homes are like in 2155.

EXPLANATION: The story starts on May 17, 2155. Tommy finds a book that is many years old. He discovers that the book is about school and explains to Margie how schools of long ago compare to the mechanical teachers of their time. **B** is correct. The sentence in which the setting is revealed lets you know immediately that students are learning from tools other than "real books."

- **A** is incorrect. The date is important, but the fact that Margie wrote it in her diary is not.
- **C** is incorrect because the date alone does not allow you to see how much education has changed.
- **D** is incorrect. Although the story takes place in Margie's home, it is not important to the story's plot.

TEKS 6A

4 Why does Margie sigh when she gives the mechanical teacher her homework?

F She is happy to be in school.

G She wonders what it would be like to learn in a schoolroom with other students.

H She wishes Tommy had left his book with her.

J She hates her mechanical teacher.

EXPLANATION: At the end of the story, Margie thinks about how different school was for her grandfather's grandfather and how much fun it must have been. **G** is correct. Margie thinks it would be fun to be with other students and have a human teacher.

- **F** is incorrect. Early in the story you learn that Margie hates school.
- **H** is incorrect. Although Margie wanted to read the book, Tommy said that he might bring it back after school.
- **J** is incorrect. Although Margie hates her mechanical teacher, she is not thinking about this when she sighs.

TEKS 6; Fig. 19D

GO ON

Name ______________________________ Date ______________

5 Margie does not want the inspector to fix the mechanical teacher because —

A she hates to put homework into the slot
B the inspector smiles and gives her an apple
C Tommy tells her that she doesn't know much
D she wants to read Tommy's book instead

EXPLANATION: Margie hates school. Margie does so poorly in geography that her mother calls an inspector to fix the mechanical teacher. **A** is correct. Margie feels the worst part of school is putting homework into the slot.

- **B** is incorrect. The text does not connect the inspector's actions with Margie's feelings about the teacher.
- **C** and **D** are incorrect. The events described in both choices happen after the inspector fixes the mechanical teacher.

TEKS 6B

6 Margie's internal conflict in paragraphs 16–30 stems from —

F her fondness for her mechanical teacher
G feeling hurt when Tommy calls her stupid
H her interest in how children learned long ago
J her arithmetic lesson on fractions

EXPLANATION: Tommy explains that long ago students had human teachers. However, Margie doesn't think that a man is smart enough to teach. Margie wants to learn more about the schools of long ago and is interested in what a human teacher would be like. **H** is correct.

- **F** is incorrect because Margie hates her mechanical teacher.
- **G** is incorrect. Margie is only momentarily hurt by Tommy's comment. She is more interested in learning about what schools were like hundreds of years ago.
- **J** is incorrect because Margie doesn't start her arithmetic lesson until the end of the story.

TEKS 6B

STOP

Reading Literary Text: Literary Nonfiction

In this part of the book, you will read a series of diary entries with instruction about the elements of literary nonfiction. Following the selection are sample questions and answers about the diary entries. The purpose of this section is to show you how to understand and analyze literary nonfiction.

To begin, review the TEKS that relate to literary nonfiction:

LITERARY NONFICTION TEKS	WHAT IT MEANS TO YOU
(7) Comprehension of Literary Text/Literary Nonfiction Students understand, make inferences and draw conclusions about the varied structural patterns and features of literary nonfiction and provide evidence from text to support their understanding. Students are expected to describe the structural and substantive differences between an autobiography or a diary and a fictional adaptation of it.	You will understand and draw conclusions about the different ways nonfiction texts are put together and support your analysis with examples from the text. You will explain the difference between an autobiography or a diary and the fictional stories based on that autobiography or diary.

The selection that follows provides instruction on the literary nonfiction TEKS as well as other TEKS. It also covers reading comprehension skills, such as making inferences and synthesizing text to make sure you understand it.

As you read the diary entries in "Celia's Experiment," notice how the author organizes and describes her thoughts. The annotations in the margins will guide you as you read.

Name ______________________ Date ____________

Guided Reading

Read this selection. Then answer the questions that follow.

Celia's Experiment

Celia is a 7th grader at a new school. Her parents worked for a company that abruptly closed down after many years. They found new jobs in a different city, so the family was forced to move in the middle of the school year. Celia writes about her new life in an old red notebook she carries in her backpack.

Date: January 12
Weather: rainy

Dear Diary,

1 Today I hesitated at the entrance to the cafeteria, not sure if I had the courage to go in. In fact, I almost went to the guidance counselor to see if I could drop lunch, maybe in exchange for another math class, which shows you just how desperate I am! Unfortunately, the library is closed during lunch periods, and the restrooms are far too grim to linger in. So, feeling like a gladiator about to face the hungry lions in the coliseum,[1] I pushed open the door. A wave of warm, moist air washed over me, smothering me with the smells of spilled ranch dressing, sour milk, and old sneakers. Edging in, I held my usual debate. Sit alone? Attach myself to a group with vaguely familiar faces? Cower behind the trash bins? In the end, I fell into the first empty spot I found, since my shaking legs wouldn't carry me any further.

2 I've been at my new school for two weeks. I still feel like a foreigner who doesn't know the language. I go through entire days without speaking unless a teacher calls on me in class. In contrast, around me the roar of conversation ebbs and flows. I catch only <u>snatches</u>, since nothing is addressed to me:

"Are you going to eat your pudding?"
"Where are we going after school, your house or mine?"
"That math test was HARD. What was Mrs. Gill thinking?"

LITERARY NONFICTION
Celia writes the date and weather for each diary entry. Pay attention to how this structural element reveals changes in Celia's thoughts and feelings as time passes and the weather improves.

TEKS 7; Fig. 19E

SENSORY LANGUAGE
Sensory language is the use of words and details that appeal to a reader's senses of sight, hearing, touch, smell, and taste. In paragraph 1, Celia uses sensory details to describe what she felt and what she smelled upon entering the cafeteria.

TEKS 7, 8; Fig. 19C

1. **gladiator . . . coliseum:** Gladiator contests were popular in ancient Rome and often took place in a circular arena called a coliseum. Most gladiators were imprisoned or enslaved men who were forced to fight other men or animals to the death as a form of entertainment.

GO ON

Name ______________________________ Date ______________

It amazes me to think that I took talking to friends for granted back home. Home—I better not go there. I miss everyone from my old life so much, especially my best friend, Mia.

Date: January 14
Weather: some wind

Dear Diary,

3 I read somewhere that it gets darkest before dawn. Well, if so, dawn better be around the corner! Things are getting pretty murky! Today, in science, we were told that we have to do a project. I love science, so that was okay with me. But then, the second part of the assignment will be to present our project to the class! As I looked around at my potential audience, I could already feel my heart pounding, my palms getting clammy, and beads of sweat forming on my forehead. I don't like public speaking at the best of times, but this could be the worst of times!

4 Of course, when I complained to Mom and Dad at dinner, Mom reminded me that by the time the project is due, I should know kids in my class. They want me to put more effort into meeting people. As Mom launched into her daily pep talk, I cleverly distracted her by asking for help with ideas for my project.

5 We came up with a plant maze. I will set some bean seeds in a little pot of soil. Then I will get an old box with a few dividers and cut one hole in each divider and a hole at each end of the box. At one end of the box, I will put the pot of seeds. At the other end, I will place a heat lamp. If my experiment works, the plants will twist through the obstacles in my maze to reach the light and warmth. Should be interesting!

Date: January 15
Weather: gray

Dear Diary,

6 This afternoon I wished the earth would open and swallow me up! As I walked out to my bus, a group of girls turned to look at me. I started to say hi, choked, and ended up having a coughing fit. I hurried past them with a face as red as one of Dad's prize tomatoes and tripped. I heard one of them laugh and another one ask what my problem was. Now I've done it! I've gone from being completely unknown to being the weird kid!! What next!

MAKING INFERENCES
In paragraph 2, you can tell that Celia doesn't mean "I'd better not go home" when she talks about missing her old home. She means "I don't want to discuss my old home."

Fig. 19D

SENSORY LANGUAGE
Figurative language is the imaginative use of words to express ideas that are not literally true. In paragraph 3, Celia does not mean that it is literally getting dark out. Instead, she uses the image of darkness to emphasize her troubled feelings.

TEKS 7, 8

LITERARY NONFICTION
Diaries are told from the first-person point of view, using the pronoun *I*. They reveal the writer's thoughts. Consider how paragraph 6 might be told in a fictional account whose narrator reports actions but doesn't tell what the characters think.

TEKS 7

GO ON

Name ______________________________ Date ______________

7 As Mom and I set up my plant maze experiment tonight, I told her about the incident at school. I think I am ready for a little advice. So, she said she was challenging me to another experiment. She wants me to introduce myself to one new kid every day. If I think of it as a scientific investigation, it seems easier to do.

Date: January 18
Weather: clouds, some sun

Dear Diary,

8 Okay—I am past my first obstacle, successfully! Today, I got to science class early and saw this tall, dark-haired girl sitting alone. So, I said hello and introduced myself. She smiled, told me her name was Angela, and invited me to sit next to her. She said that she just moved here last year! I never would have guessed. Angela introduced me to Jesse, Kate, and Ty. They all seem nice. Suddenly, instead of the room being a sea of strangers, there are a few islands of friendly faces.

Date: February 15
Weather: warm breezes

Dear Diary,

9 My science presentation is tomorrow! My plants made their way over and around the obstacles in their path, adapting when necessary—like me, I guess. We've all reached our goals by taking one step at a time and not giving up. After writing my report on my plants, I talked with Mom about how much happier I am at school. I've learned some important lessons from both my experiments . . . Well, Angela is expecting me to call her, so I'll write more later!

CONTEXT CLUES
When you come across an unfamiliar word, such as *incident* in paragraph 7, look for clues in surrounding sentences to find its meaning. The phrase "at school" provides a clue that *incident* refers to the event that Celia described in paragraph 6.

TEKS 2B

SENSORY LANGUAGE
A metaphor makes an indirect comparison between two unlike things that have some qualities in common. In paragraph 8, Celia no longer feels overwhelmed by her class because there are now "islands" of familiar faces among the "sea of strangers."

TEKS 7, 8

LITERARY NONFICTION
According to the date of this entry (paragraph 9), more than a month has passed since Celia's first entry. Notice that the warm, pleasant weather coincides with the change in her feelings.

TEKS 7; Fig. 19E

GO ON

Name ______________________________ Date ______________

Use "Celia's Experiment" (pp. 13–15) to answer questions 1–7.

1 Which of the following best describes how Celia's feelings change between January and February as the weather improves?

A She is enthusiastic at first but then begins to miss her old school.

B She has a difficult start but eventually becomes more comfortable.

C She is nervous at first, and things worsen when she is unable to make any friends.

D She has a positive start and gains more confidence from the success of her experiments.

EXPLANATION: Celia feels uncomfortable at her new school at first but begins to feel better about her situation as she makes friends and works on her science project. **B** is correct.

- **A** is incorrect. In her first entry, Celia describes being very nervous and shy and missing her old life terribly.
- **C** is incorrect. Although Celia is nervous at first, her situation improves as she makes friends.
- **D** is incorrect. Although Celia gains confidence from success with her experiments, her experiences at the beginning are negative, not positive.

TEKS 7; Fig. 19E

2 Based on the sensory details Celia provides in paragraph 1, how did she most likely feel upon entering the cafeteria?

F Dizzy and faint

G Excited and eager

H Exhausted and hungry

J Reluctant and queasy

EXPLANATION: Celia describes warm air enveloping her with unpleasant smells. She is reluctant to enter the cafeteria. **J** is correct.

- **F** is incorrect. Although Celia may have experienced dizziness and faintness as a result of her nervousness, the warm air and unpleasant smells would not necessarily cause these feelings.
- **G** is incorrect. The details suggest that Celia felt hesitant and rather sick, not excited and eager.
- **H** is incorrect. The details do not suggest exhaustion, and she would most likely be too revolted by the smells to feel hungry.

TEKS 7, 8; Fig. 19D

GO ON

Name ______________________________ Date ______________

3 Read the following dictionary entry.

> **snatch** \snăch\ *n.* **1.** the act of grabbing or grasping **2.** a short period of time **3.** a bit or piece of something **4.** *slang* a kidnapping

What is the definition of snatch as it is used in paragraph 2?

A Definition 1

B Definition 2

C Definition 3

D Definition 4

EXPLANATION: Celia refers to and gives examples of the pieces of conversations she overhears. From the context, you can tell that a *snatch* is a small amount. **C** is correct.

- **A** is incorrect. The context does not suggest an act of grabbing or grasping.
- **B** is incorrect. A short period of time does not make sense within the sentence, since Celia uses a colon to introduce examples of the bits of conversation she overhears.
- **D** is incorrect. A kidnapping does not relate to Celia's entry.

TEKS 2B, 2E

4 Based on Celia's description in paragraph 4, what can you conclude about how Celia regards her mother's pep talk?

F Celia dismisses her mother's ability to help with her social problems.

G The talk makes Celia feel encouraged about meeting new friends.

H Celia doesn't care about making friends and only wants to talk about her science project.

J The talk makes Celia resent being forced to move away from her friends.

EXPLANATION: Celia is interested in advice on her science project and doesn't take her mother's pep talk seriously. **F** is correct.

- **G** is incorrect. Celia doesn't seem to pay attention to the talk and focuses her concern on her science project.
- **H** is incorrect. Celia does care about making friends, but she doubts that listening to her mother's pep talk will help her.
- **J** is incorrect. No details suggest that Celia is resentful.

TEKS 7; Fig. 19D

GO ON

Name ______________________________ Date ______________

5 In paragraph 8, Celia describes a scene in her science class. In a fictional film adaptation of this diary entry, which element of the entry is least likely to be acted out?

A *Okay—I am past my first obstacle, successfully!*

B *I said hello and introduced myself.*

C *She smiled, told me her name was Angela, and invited me to sit next to her.*

D *Angela introduced me to Jesse, Kate, and Ty.*

EXPLANATION: Diary entries reveal a writer's thoughts and feelings and use the pronoun *I*. A film adaptation would show what all the characters do and say, but it would not necessarily reveal their thoughts. **A** is correct.

- **B**, **C**, and **D** are incorrect. The dialogue and actions suggested in these lines would be relatively easy to translate to the screen.

TEKS 7

6 The word obstacle is used in paragraph 5 and again in paragraph 8 to mean —

F someone who stands in the way

G something that prevents progress

H a challenge that a person overcomes

J a physical barrier that prevents movement

EXPLANATION: An *obstacle* is something that prevents progress, either literally or figuratively. **G** is correct. In paragraph 5, dividers act as physical obstacles in Celia's plant maze. In paragraph 8, the obstacle is the personal challenge that Celia overcomes by introducing herself to a girl in her class.

- **F** is incorrect. The word is not used to describe a person in either context.
- **H** is incorrect. The word is used in this way only in paragraph 8.
- **J** is incorrect. The word is used in this way only in paragraph 5.

TEKS 2B

7 What lessons does Celia learn from both of her experiments?

A Plants are more adaptable than people.

B Plants continue to grow but people do not.

C Both mazes and moves can prevent opportunities and growth.

D Both plants and people can adapt to challenges and change.

EXPLANATION: In Celia's science experiment, the plants went over and around the obstacles to reach the heat lamp. In Celia's personal experiment, she overcame her nervousness and shyness about introducing herself to new people. **D** is correct.

- **A** is incorrect. Both Celia and her plants were able to adapt.
- **B** is incorrect. There is no indication that Celia will stop growing and changing.
- **C** is incorrect. The maze did not prevent the plant from growing, and Celia's move gave her new opportunities to grow.

TEKS 7; Fig. 19B

STOP

Reading Literary Text: Poetry

In this part of the book, you will read a poem with instruction about the elements of poetry. Following the selection are sample questions and answers about the poem. The purpose of this section is to show you how to understand and analyze poetry.

To begin, review the TEKS that relate to poetry:

POETRY TEKS	WHAT IT MEANS TO YOU
(4) Comprehension of Literary Text/Poetry Students understand, make inferences and draw conclusions about the structure and elements of poetry and provide evidence from text to support their understanding. Students are expected to analyze the importance of graphical elements (e.g., capital letters, line length, word position) on the meaning of a poem.	You will analyze the ways in which poems are put together and use examples from the poem to explain your analysis. You will analyze how the visual elements of a poem affect the poem's meaning.

The selection that follows provides instruction on the poetry TEKS as well as other TEKS. It also covers reading comprehension skills, such as using sensory language to visualize the meaning of a poem.

As you read the poem "International News," notice how the poet uses both words and the placement of those words to convey meaning. The annotations in the margin will guide you as you read.

Name ______________________________ Date ______________

Guided Reading

Read this selection. Then answer the questions that follow.

International News

On August 5, 2010, a coal mine in Copiacó, Chile, collapsed. Thirty-three miners were trapped more than 2,000 feet below ground. The massive rescue operation involved drilling a narrow shaft for a rescue capsule. When drillers finally broke through to the miners, each man made a twenty-minute solo journey to the surface. The miners were all rescued after 69 days underground.

The first report said,
"Miners trapped
deep
beneath
the earth,"

a roof of rock, a sky of soil,
two thousand feet
thick
between them
and sunlight.

One week, two weeks, then a message from below:
"Estamos bien
en el refugio los 33."[1]
"We're OK!"

Hope fed faith
six long weeks,
waiting . . . praying . . . watching . . . worrying . . .

Until today.
Each man emerged
from the rescue pod
as if stepping onto the dust
of a distant moon.
Sixty-six arms reaching out to hug and hold,
Exchanging dark for light,
fear for love,
despair for life.

1. **Estamos bien en el refugio los 33:** Spanish for "We are alright in the shelter, the 33 of us."

SENSORY LANGUAGE
Line 6 uses a metaphor to compare the tons of soil above the miners to the sky. Keeping in mind the vastness of the sky, think how this comparison affects your understanding of the miners' situation.

TEKS 4, 8; Fig. 19C

POETRY
The arrangement of words and lines on a page reinforces a poem's meaning. Notice the length of line 17. The words are spread out, showing how slowly time passes for those on the surface hoping for good news about the rescue operation.

TEKS 4

CONTEXT CLUES
To define an unfamiliar word, such as *pod* in line 20, use the words and phrases around it. The word *emerged,* which means "came out," suggests that a pod is a vehicle of some kind, probably compact to enable it to reach so far below the earth's surface.

TEKS 2B

GO ON

Name ______________________ Date ______________

Use "International News" (p. 20) to answer questions 1–4.

1 Which of these elements creates a visual image of how deep in the earth the miners are?

A The ellipses in line 17
B The length of lines 11 and 23
C The repetition of *r* and *s* sounds in line 6
D The arrangement of words in lines 1–14

EXPLANATION: To reinforce the image of how far below the surface the miners are, the poet stacks the words in the first three stanzas vertically. The reader's eye can then sense the words' meaning. **D** is correct.

- **A** is incorrect. The ellipses signal pauses. In this line, the use of ellipses suggests both that people are breathless with anticipation as they await news and that the planning of the rescue takes a very long time.
- **B** is incorrect. In line 11, the length of the line shows how long it takes to receive word from the miners that they are okay. In line 23, the length of the line might reflect the action of arms reaching out.
- **C** is incorrect. The alliteration in this line does not by itself create an understanding of how deep the damaged mine is.

TEKS 4

2 In lines 19–22, the miners walk from the rescue pod as if they are "stepping onto the dust / of a distant moon." Through this simile, the poet conveys the —

F cold, dark setting
G miners' feelings of wonder at their survival
H men's resemblance to astronauts
J exhaustion of the miners after their ordeal

EXPLANATION: The first astronauts who walked on the moon felt amazement at their feat. The miners feel similar emotions as they reach the surface. Therefore, the simile is used to convey their sense of wonder and awe that they have survived their ordeal. **G** is correct.

- **F** and **H** are incorrect. The focus of the simile is on the men's actions, not the physical site of their rescue or their clothing.
- **J** is incorrect. The simile offers no insights into the men's physical condition.

TEKS 4, 8

GO ON

Name ______________________________ Date ______________

3 An antonym, or word that means the opposite, of despair in line 26 is —

A sadness
B pride
C hope
D laughter

EXPLANATION: In lines 24–26, the miners are exchanging negative feelings for positive. Therefore, the opposite of despair is a feeling that is positive. **C** is correct. Hope is always a positive emotion, no matter the circumstances.

- **A** is incorrect. Sadness is a negative emotion and cannot be the opposite of another negative emotion.
- **B** is incorrect. Pride is not always a positive quality or emotion.
- **D** is incorrect. Laughter can express many different emotions but is not a feeling in itself.

TEKS 2B

4 Which of the following is the best paraphrase of lines 15–17?

F People were comforted by hope and faith as they waited six weeks for the miners' rescue.
G The miners' family members were so worried that they could not eat, but their hope kept them alive.
H Without hope, there can be no faith, especially when people we love are in danger.
J After six weeks of waiting, praying, and watching, people of faith could only worry about the miners.

EXPLANATION: These lines suggest that as people waited to hear about the miners, their hope and faith kept them going. **F** is correct.

- **G** is incorrect. The word *fed* in line 15 does not refer to eating food; it is used figuratively to mean that people's attitude of hope prevented them from losing faith that the miners would be rescued.
- **H** is incorrect. Lines 15–17 describe the families' six-week vigil, not a universal statement about hope and faith.
- **J** is incorrect. The order of words in line 17 does not suggest that people did these things in sequence, with worrying happening last.

Fig. 19E

STOP

Reading Literary Text: Drama

In this part of the book, you will read a short play with instruction about the elements of drama. Following the selection are sample questions and answers about the play. The purpose of this section is to show you how to understand and analyze drama.

To begin, review the TEKS that relate to dramatic texts:

DRAMA TEKS	WHAT IT MEANS TO YOU
(5) Comprehension of Literary Text/Drama Students understand, make inferences and draw conclusions about the structure and elements of drama and provide evidence from text to support their understanding. Students are expected to explain a playwright's use of dialogue and stage directions.	You will understand and draw conclusions about the ways dramas are put together and support your analysis with examples from the text. You will discuss how playwrights use dialogue and stage directions to convey meaning in a drama.

The selection that follows provides instruction on the drama TEKS as well as other TEKS. It also covers reading comprehension skills, such as making inferences and reflecting on your understanding of text.

As you read the play "The Dream of Good Fortune," notice how the playwright uses the literary elements described above. The annotations in the margins will guide you as you read.

Name ______________________________ Date ______________

Guided Reading

Read this selection. Then answer the questions that follow.

The Dream of Good Fortune

from The Arabian Nights, *dramatized by Paul Sills*

This drama takes place long ago in the Middle East. The main character, Luqman Ali, lives in Baghdad, which was the center of Islamic civilization during the period in which many of the Arabian Nights *stories are set. In the play, "Luq" is an abbreviation for "Luqman Ali." He travels to Cairo, in Egypt.*

CHARACTERS

Luqman Ali	The Chief of Police
His Wife	A Thief
An Angel	The Lieutenant

Luq. Luqman Ali, a poor but honest dung sweeper, lived in the alley of the tanners, off the street of the potters,[1] in the heart of the great city of Baghdad.

Wife. He and his wife had nothing in the world but an old iron stove, and barely enough to eat.

Luq. But still they did not despair in the mercy of the Almighty. One night Luqman Ali and his wife lay down to sleep, and he had a dream.

Angel. An angel appeared with a message: "Luqman Ali, alley of the tanners, off the street of the potters, in the city of Baghdad—Dear Luq, Go to Cairo, and there you will find your fortune."

ELEMENTS OF DRAMA
A play is told through dialogue, or conversation between characters. Each character's name is identified in bold type. In the first few lines, Luqman Ali, his wife, and the angel also act as narrators, setting the scene by talking about themselves in the third person. Notice that other characters do this later in the play.

TEKS 5

1. **tanners . . . potters:** Tanners are people who make animal hides into leather; potters are people who make pots and dishes out of clay.

GO ON

Name ____________________ Date ____________

Luq. Luqman Ali awoke his wife and told her of his strange dream.

Wife. Go back to sleep, my love, it was only a dream.

Angel. Luqman Ali, go to Cairo, and there you will find your fortune.

Luq. Wife, wake up; the angel came again and told me to go to Cairo, to seek my fortune.

Wife. If it happens a third time, you'll have to go.

Angel. Luqman Ali, are you still here? Go to Cairo! Your fortune awaits you there.

Luq. I go! I go! Wife, awaken—I must go to Cairo. And so Luqman Ali set off on the road to Cairo. Through hot desert winds—sandstorms—cold nights. Luqman Ali traveled the road until, weary and sore, in the shimmering heat, he saw the great city of Cairo. Tired and not knowing where to go, he took refuge in the courtyard of a great mosque,[2] where he lay down to sleep.

Thief. That night, a thief entered the courtyard and broke through the wall of an adjoining house.

[*A woman screams offstage. The* THIEF *returns to the courtyard, hits* LUQ, *and runs off.*]

Luq. Stop, thief! Stop, thief!

Chief of Police. The chief of police . . .

Lieutenant. And his lieutenant . . .

Chief of Police. Arrived at the scene, and they found Luqman Ali, and thinking him to be the thief . . .

Lieutenant. They beat him with their clubs and dragged him off to jail.

Chief of Police. Who are you?

Luq. Luqman Ali.

Chief of Police. Where do you come from?

Luq. Baghdad.

CONTEXT CLUES
When you find an unfamiliar word, such as *refuge,* look for clues in the words around it to figure out its meaning. The phrase "not knowing where to go" can help you figure out that *refuge* is a safe place for Luqman Ali to sleep.

TEKS 2B

STAGE DIRECTIONS
Some lines are in italics and enclosed within parentheses or brackets. These are stage directions, which describe actions that are not revealed in the dialogue.

TEKS 5

ELEMENTS OF DRAMA
Like any story, a play has a conflict, or struggle, for the main character. Luqman Ali is arrested and cannot prove that he is not the thief. This has created a conflict by keeping him from finding his fortune.

TEKS 5

2. **mosque:** a place of worship for followers of the Islamic faith.

GO ON

Chief of Police. What brings you to Cairo?

Luq. I had a dream . . .

[*The* LIEUTENANT *squeezes* LUQ*'s nose, sending him to his knees.*]

Chief of Police. What are you doing in Cairo?

Luq (*rises*). I had a dream...

[*The* LIEUTENANT *squeezes his head.*]

Chief of Police (*waving the* LIEUTENANT *away*). What brings you to Cairo?

Luq (*again on his knees*). I had a dream. An angel appeared to me three times in a row and told me to go to Cairo, where I would find my fortune.

Chief of Police. And what did you find?

Luq. I got arrested and beat up.

Chief of Police. It hurts too, doesn't it? Dreams mean nothing. We all have dreams. You fool! That's the trouble with you people. Superstitious. I had a dream only last night: An angel came to me and told me to go to Baghdad, to the alley of the potters, off the street of the tanners, to a little old shack, and there under an old iron stove I would find a treasure. Did I go? No! I stayed here doing my job. Here, take these dinars[3] and get out of here.

[*So* LUQ *sets off to his home in Baghdad. He "dances" back to Baghdad, calling "Wife, wife." They move the stove, find the treasure, and adorn each other with jewels. She kisses his nose.—"Owww!!!"—Fade Out.*]

ELEMENTS OF DRAMA
At a play's climax, you learn how the conflict will be resolved. The climax occurs when it seems Luqman Ali has failed to find his good fortune.

TEKS 5

ELEMENTS OF DRAMA
The resolution wraps up the play and tells you what happens to the characters. The chief of police's dream helps resolve Luqman Ali's problem by revealing where Luqman can find the fortune.

TEKS 5

3. **dinars:** gold coins used in ancient Arab countries.

GO ON

Name ________________________________ Date ____________

Use "The Dream of Good Fortune" (pp. 24–26) to answer questions 1–6.

1 Why does Luqman Ali go to Cairo?

A The angel orders him to go.
B He wants to find the potters.
C His wife asks him to go.
D He wants to find his fortune.

> **EXPLANATION:** Review the dialogue at the beginning of the play. **D** is correct because an angel appears to Luqman Ali in a dream and tells him to go to Cairo to find his fortune.
> - **A** is incorrect because the angel does not order him to go.
> - **B** is incorrect because it describes where Luqman Ali is living in Baghdad.
> - **C** is incorrect. His wife supports his decision, but she does not ask him to go.

TEKS 5

2 In which lines does Luqman Ali act as both a character and a narrator in the play?

F *I go! I go!*
G *I must go to Cairo. And so Luqman Ali set off on the road to Cairo.*
H *Through hot desert winds—sandstorms—cold nights.*
J *Luqman Ali traveled the road until, weary and sore, in the shimmering heat, he saw the great city of Cairo.*

> **EXPLANATION:** Characters use the first-person pronoun "I" in dialogue; they use the third person when acting as a narrator. **G** is correct because in the first line, the pronoun "I" indicates that Luqman Ali is speaking as a character in dialogue. In the second line, he refers to himself as "Luqman Ali," indicating that he is now acting as a narrator.
> - **F** is incorrect because the pronoun "I" indicates that Luqman Ali is speaking as a character in dialogue.
> - **H** and **J** are incorrect because the lines are descriptions of the scene provided by Luqman Ali as a narrator.

TEKS 5; Fig. 19D

3 What does the word <u>adjoining</u> mean in line 31?

A Connected
B Fancy
C Old
D Distant

> **EXPLANATION:** When you analyze a word's parts, such as its prefix, root, and suffix, you must also consider how the word is used in the line. The context of the line suggests that the thief broke into a nearby house. **A** is correct because the prefix *ad-* means "near" and the word part *joining* means "connect."
> - **B** and **C** are incorrect because there is no evidence in the play that the house is fancy or old.
> - **D** is incorrect because *distant* is an antonym, or the opposite, of *adjoining*.

TEKS 2A

GO ON

Name ______________________ Date ______________

4 From his interaction with Luqman Ali, you learn that the chief of police —

F does not believe that dreams can come true

G does not believe in angels

H treats all of his prisoners badly

J thinks people from Baghdad are superstitious

EXPLANATION: When Luqman Ali tells the chief of police about his dream, the chief says, "Dreams mean nothing." **F** is correct because the chief of police makes fun of Luqman Ali for traveling to Cairo because of a dream.

- **G** is incorrect because the chief does not say what he thinks about angels.
- **H** is incorrect because there is no evidence in the play that the chief treats all of his prisoners badly.
- **J** is incorrect because the chief states that "you people" are superstitious. He doesn't refer directly to people from Baghdad.

TEKS 5; Fig. 19D

5 In the stage directions in line 67, Luqman Ali "'dances' back to Baghdad" because he —

A has been released from jail

B is excited to see his wife

C is eager to leave Cairo

D knows the location of the fortune

EXPLANATION: This question asks you to make an inference, or logical guess, about why Luqman Ali is dancing. When you make an inference, you consider evidence from the text and your own experiences. **D** is correct because Luqman Ali has learned from the chief of police's dream that the fortune is under the stove in his house in Baghdad.

- **A, B,** and **C** are incorrect. Luqman Ali is probably happy to be released from jail, excited to see his wife, and eager to leave Cairo, but those are not the main reasons he is dancing back to Baghdad.

TEKS 5; Fig. 19D

6 What theme or message does the play convey?

F It is dangerous to travel to other countries.

G You should beware of police in other countries.

H You can follow your dreams to find good fortune.

J Dreams that occur three times will come true.

EXPLANATION: A theme is a message about life or human nature that the writer wants you to understand. In most cases, you need to infer the theme by finding clues in the text. **H** is correct. Luqman Ali and his wife are very poor at the beginning of the play; however, they follow their dreams and find a fortune.

- **F** is incorrect. Cairo is a setting in the play, but it does not relate to the theme of the play.
- **G** is incorrect. Luqman Ali's trouble with the police is the conflict, not the theme, in the play.
- **J** is incorrect. Luqman Ali's wife tells him he must travel to Cairo if he has the same dream three times. However, this is a plot event to build suspense, not the message of the play.

TEKS 3; Fig. 19D

STOP

Reading Informational Text: Expository Text

In this part of the book, you will read an informational article with instruction about the elements of expository text. Following the selection are sample questions and answers about the article. The purpose of this section is to show you how to understand and analyze expository text.

To begin, review the TEKS that relate to expository text:

EXPOSITORY TEXT TEKS	WHAT IT MEANS TO YOU
(10) Comprehension of Informational Text/Expository Text Students analyze, make inferences and draw conclusions about expository text and provide evidence from text to support their understanding. Students are expected to:	
(A) evaluate a summary of the original text for accuracy of the main ideas, supporting details, and overall meaning;	You will analyze the summary of a text to see how accurate it is in capturing the text's main idea, meaning, and important details.
(B) distinguish factual claims from commonplace assertions and opinions;	You will tell the difference between statements of fact and opinions or assumptions.
(C) use different organizational patterns as guides for summarizing and forming an overview of different kinds of expository text; and	You will use different types of organization to create summaries and overviews of a text.
(D) synthesize and make logical connections between ideas within a text and across two or three texts representing similar or different genres, and support those findings with textual evidence.	You will make connections between multiple ideas found in one text or similar ideas found in different kinds of texts and support those connections with evidence.

The selection that follows provides instruction on the expository text TEKS as well as other TEKS. It also covers reading comprehension skills, such as synthesizing and summarizing information to better understand a text.

As you read the article "It Could Happen to You," notice how the author organizes and presents information. The annotations in the margins will guide you as you read.

Name ______________________________ Date ______________

Guided Reading

Read this selection. Then answer the questions that follow.

It Could Happen to You

1 It is a human-made monster. No one can escape the reach of its tentacles, which can extend not just across a room but also around the entire planet. It gets worse. This monster, known by names such as the Brain, Crusher, Grog, and the Creeper, can quickly reproduce and shut down entire systems. This is no science fiction or fantasy creature. It's a computer virus.

2 The effects of computer viruses range from pesky system crashes to life-threatening situations. Regardless of the results of a virus, it should never be taken lightly. A computer virus is generally defined as a self-replicating program that inserts itself into other programs stored on a computer. Some viruses may be relatively harmless, but most are designed to have negative consequences, such as destroying the computer's operating system (the basic software that runs the computer), corrupting the computer's memory, or causing other programs to stop functioning. The term *self-replicating* is a clue to how a virus is able to cause so much damage. It keeps making copies of itself over and over again.

3 Here's an explanation of how a computer virus works, based on a model by the computer scientist Eugene Kaspersky.

4 A teacher is working at his desk at the end of the day. He finds mistakes in the midterm answer key, so he tosses it into the trash. Because the trash can is overflowing, the answer key falls onto the floor.

5 Then the teacher feels a headache coming on and goes home. The custodian comes to empty the trash, sees the answer key on the floor, and picks it up. He puts it back on the teacher's desk. But now, attached to the answer key is a sticky note that says, "Copy two times, and put copies in other teachers' boxes."

MAIN IDEA
The main idea of a paragraph may be stated directly, or it may be implied by the details that the writer includes. The details in paragraph 1 help readers infer the writer's main idea: A computer virus is both frightening and powerful.

Fig. 19D

CONTEXT CLUES
Sometimes the definition of an unfamiliar word is restated in the sentences that follow it. For example, the last sentence of paragraph 2 is an explanation of the term *self-replicating*.

TEKS 2B

SYNTHESIZING
Starting in paragraph 4, the writer presents an analogy—a comparison to something with which readers are familiar—to explain how a computer virus spreads. This analogy helps you visualize more clearly what happens inside a computer when it is infected by a virus.

TEKS 10D; Fig. 19C

GO ON

Name ______________________ Date ____________

6 The next day the teacher stays home because he has the flu. As a result, a substitute is called to the school. The first thing the substitute sees is the answer key with the note stuck to it. So, she copies it twice for each teacher and puts the copies in the teachers' boxes. She leaves the sticky note on the answer key so they will see that the absent teacher wanted them to get the copies.

7 When the other teachers find the two copies of the answer key with the instructions to copy them twice and distribute them, they give them to the office clerk. She then makes more copies of the answer key and puts them into the boxes of the "other teachers." By the end of the day, the school is out of paper, and the teachers' boxes are stuffed with useless answer keys.

SUMMARIZING
To make sure you understand what you are reading, pause at intervals and summarize the key ideas in your own words. For example, after reading paragraph 7, you might say, "The clerk makes four copies of the answer key for each teacher."

TEKS 10A; Fig. 19C, 19E

8 As illustrated in the chart, each replication of the answer key produces more and more copies until the process is stopped because someone realizes what is happening or because the supply of paper runs out. Similarly, a computer virus increases by leaps and bounds, taking over, until the system breaks down or the user finds a way to remove it.

Cause: Two copies of the answer key with the sticky-note instructions still included are distributed to each teacher.

↓

Effect/Cause: Following the directions, double copies are made of each set of two answer keys and distributed to all teachers.

↓

Effect/Cause: Double copies of the four answer keys in each mailbox are made and handed out to all teachers.

↓

Effect: Finally, chaos erupts; paper runs out; mailboxes are overloaded.

GRAPHIC ORGANIZER
Graphic organizers enable readers to see the relationships among ideas more clearly. In this chart, notice how each effect becomes the cause of another event until the last effect.

TEKS 12B

GO ON

Name ______________________________ Date ______________

9 This model resembles what happens with a computer virus. The difference between the answer-key situation and a computer virus lies in motivation. The teacher didn't plan to cause chaos in the school. The whole mess was just a series of unfortunate causes and effects. On the other hand, computer viruses are created by people who have all kinds of motives, none of them good. The effects are the corruption of massive amounts of important information as well as the cost of billions of dollars in lost productivity every year.

10 Developers of antivirus programs are gaining on the virus villains, making it easier to detect a virus before it spreads and causes a wave of destruction. Most computers today come with antivirus programs that can be updated automatically in order to detect new threats. Nonetheless, watch what you put in your computer . . . and in your trash.

PATTERNS OF ORGANIZATION
To explain the analogy between a virus and a teacher's misplaced trash, the writer uses a cause-and-effect pattern to organize the details. However, other paragraphs have a different organizational pattern. In paragraph 9, the phrase *on the other hand* signals the use of comparison and contrast.

TEKS 10C

GO ON

Name ________________________________ Date ______________

Use "It Could Happen to You" (pp. 30–32) to answer questions 1–7.

1 Which words and phrases from the selection signal the organizational pattern used by the writer in the analogy to the misplaced answer key?

A *but, on the other hand, similarly*

B *the next day, then, by the end of the day*

C *so, because, as a result*

D *such as, and, or*

EXPLANATION: This analogy shows how a computer virus disrupts the operation of a computer by discussing the causes and effects of the replication process. **C** is correct. These words and phrases signal a cause-and-effect pattern.

- **A** is incorrect. These words and phrases are used to signal comparison and contrast.
- **B** is incorrect. These words indicate a chronological order.
- **D** is incorrect. These words and phrases are used to introduce examples that develop the main idea.

TEKS 10C

2 Based on the details in this selection, the reader could infer that —

F getting rid of a virus can be difficult

G the majority of viruses are created accidentally

H viruses have limited potential to cause harm

J most people would not notice that their computer has been infected with a virus

EXPLANATION: The details stress the thorough way in which a virus invades and takes over a computer. This leads readers to infer that, once established, a virus may be hard to get rid of. **F** is correct.

- **G** is incorrect. In paragraph 9, the writer states that computer viruses are intentionally created.
- **H** is incorrect. The opposite appears to be true, based on the description of the self-replication process.
- **J** is incorrect. It is possible that a virus might escape detection for a while, but the selection suggests that at some point, the computer will no longer be able to carry out its functions, causing the user to notice the problem.

Fig. 19D

GO ON

3 The best synonym, or word with a similar meaning, for corruption as it is used in paragraph 9 is —

A improvement
B change
C spoiling
D dishonesty

EXPLANATION: Context clues in paragraph 9, such as *chaos, mess,* and *lost productivity,* help identify the meaning of *corruption* as "spoiling," in the sense of being damaged. **C** is correct.

- **A** and **B** are incorrect. The context clues suggest that *corruption* is negative. *Improvement* is not a negative word, and *change* can be either positive or negative.
- **D** is incorrect. Although dishonesty is associated with corruption, it does not fit the context of this sentence.

TEKS 2B

4 A real virus takes over cells in a living body so that they create more viruses. How does knowing this fact help you understand how a computer virus works?

F A computer virus works like a real virus because it is self-replicating.
G A computer's hard drive has a structure that is very similar to a living cell.
H Unlike a real virus, a computer virus cannot make people sick.
J Both kinds of viruses are dangerous and make people nervous.

EXPLANATION: The self-replicating nature of computer viruses is what allows them to damage people's computers. **F** is correct. By synthesizing this fact about real viruses, you can better understand the way computer viruses work.

- **G** is incorrect. A computer and a living cell have very different structures.
- **H** is incorrect. While this statement is true, it does not connect the ways in which real viruses and computer viruses work.
- **J** is incorrect. This statement may be true, but it does not help you understand how computer viruses work.

TEKS 10D

GO ON

Name ______________________________ Date ______________

5 Which of the following is the best summary of this selection?

A Computers must be protected from viruses. Some viruses cause a lot of damage. Others do not.

B Computer viruses are self-replicating, which enables them to spread quickly throughout a computer. The damage they cause can be extremely serious.

C A computer virus is like copying the wrong answer key many times. Only running out of paper stops the replication process.

D The computer age has introduced a new threat—the computer virus. This virus is monstrous and destructive. Nothing can stop it.

EXPLANATION: A summary states the key ideas of the selection in order. This selection explains the self-replicating nature of computer viruses and describes the impact of this process on a computer. Therefore, **B** is correct.

- **A** is incorrect. These points are stated or implied in the selection but do not express the main ideas.
- **C** is incorrect. Although the analogy of copying the wrong answer key is used to help explain self-replication, it is not the main idea of the selection.
- **D** is incorrect. Computer viruses are monstrous in some ways, but the selection does not state that they cannot be stopped.

TEKS 10A; Fig. 19C, 19E

6 What is the specific function of the chart in this selection?

F To illustrate what happens when a teacher takes a sick day

G To convey the lesson that it is necessary to read directions carefully

H To explain the motives of someone who introduces a virus into a computer

J To show how a computer virus can very quickly grow out of control

EXPLANATION: The chart focuses on the increase in the number of copies that each distribution causes. **J** is correct. The chart helps readers understand how quickly a virus replicates and takes over a computer.

- **F** and **G** are incorrect. The chart uses the example of answer keys to illustrate the virus replication process. The relationship to the school setting is irrelevant.
- **H** is incorrect. No information is given in the chart about a "hacker's" motives.

TEKS 12B

7 Which of these statements supports the main idea of paragraph 10?

A Today's antivirus programs are more effective than ever.

B If your computer won't turn off, it may have a virus.

C Shredding important documents is a good idea.

D Experts specializing in ways to prevent viruses know a lot about computers.

EXPLANATION: The main idea of the last paragraph is that virus detection and prevention methods are improving. **A** is correct. The fact that most computers come with antivirus programs supports this idea.

- **B, C,** and **D** are incorrect. All of these statements may be true, but they do not support or relate to the key idea of the paragraph.

TEKS 10A

STOP

Reading Informational Text: Persuasive Text

In this part of the book, you will read a short speech with instruction about persuasive text. Following the selection are sample questions and answers about the speech. The purpose of this section is to show you how to understand and analyze persuasive text.

To begin, review the TEKS that relate to persuasive text:

PERSUASIVE TEXT TEKS	WHAT IT MEANS TO YOU
(11) Comprehension of Informational Text/Persuasive Text Students analyze, make inferences and draw conclusions about persuasive text and provide evidence from text to support their analysis. Students are expected to:	
(A) analyze the structure of the central argument in contemporary policy speeches (e.g., argument by cause and effect, analogy, authority) and identify the different types of evidence used to support the argument; and	You will analyze the way policy speeches are structured and identify the evidence used to support a speech's main argument.
(B) identify such rhetorical fallacies as ad hominem, exaggeration, stereotyping, or categorical claims in persuasive texts.	You will identify when poor reasoning or fallacies, such as ad hominem, exaggeration, stereotyping, or categorical claims, are used in a persuasive text.

The selection that follows provides instruction on the persuasive text TEKS as well as other TEKS. It also covers reading comprehension skills, such as asking evaluative questions about text.

As you read the speech "One Hundred Trees, Please," notice how the speaker organizes and supports the argument. The annotations in the margins will guide you as you read.

Name ______________________________ Date ______________

Guided Reading

Read this selection. Then answer the questions that follow.

One Hundred Trees, Please

A student delivered this speech at a Student Council meeting in an effort to win support for a recycling program at her school.

1 Fellow members of the student council, I want to speak to you today about the importance of starting a school-wide paper recycling program. With such a program, we can help not only our school community but also the whole world.

2 Students throughout the country use reams of paper daily. We take notes in class on paper. We submit our homework on paper. We print pages of information from the Internet—on paper. Too often, all of these sheets end up being thrown out. Even in this computer-driven age, we go through paper as if it grows on trees! Of course, paper does grow on trees. It is a product of wood—fortunately, one that is inexpensive. But, while the price of paper may be low, the environmental cost of paper production is high. We need to begin a recycling program to stop the damage to our planet before it's too late to save it.

3 Scientists estimate that, in prehistoric times, forests flourished on about 60 percent of the earth's surface. Today, about 30 percent of the earth is covered with forests. Anyone who doubts that our increased demand for paper has caused this decrease in trees should have his or her head examined. For example, just at our school alone, we use approximately six tons of paper annually. Each ton requires the destruction of seventeen oxygen-producing trees. So, recycling our six tons of paper could save over one hundred trees a year—almost an entire forest. Clearly, recycling paper would help us all breathe more easily.

RHETORICAL FALLACY
Exaggeration is an example of rhetorical fallacy, or unsound reasoning, often used in persuasive text. In paragraph 1, the speaker exaggerates the impact of a school-wide recycling program.

TEKS 11B

CONTEXT CLUES
If you don't know the word *environmental* in paragraph 2, look for context clues in surrounding sentences. The phrases "paper does grow on trees" and "to stop the damage to our planet" can help you figure out that *environmental* means "relating to natural surroundings."

TEKS 2B

ARGUMENT
Solid arguments can be supported by appealing to authorities, such as experts. By referring to scientific estimates in paragraph 3, the writer strengthens her argument.

TEKS 11A; Fig. 19B

GO ON

Name ________________________________ Date ______________

4 Recycling would also cut down on the amount of trash that must be taken to and then buried in waste disposal sites. Paper is biodegradable, meaning it should break down over time. Landfills, however, do not have the necessary exposure to water, oxygen, and sunlight to make this process happen. In some landfills, researchers have found stacks of newspapers buried for fifty years that have barely started to decompose.

5 Recycling does have its skeptics. These whiners claim that recycling paper is too much trouble and too expensive. In fact, the opposite is true. According to Marjorie Lamb, author of *2 Minutes a Day for a Greener Planet,* "saving paper is one of the easiest and most beneficial contributions we can make to our environment." Across town, North Lake Middle School started a successful paper-recycling program last year. In each classroom the teacher has a box for white paper. All the students have to do is throw white paper into the box and other trash into the regular trash can. The teacher's job is easy, too. At the end of the week, he or she simply sends a student to empty the box into one of the school's fifteen recycling containers. These containers, which are just trash cans marked "white paper only," cost the school less than $150. At the end of the week, the janitors take the recycling cans outside, where the city collects them at no charge. For the cost of a few trash cans, we can and should start our own paper-recycling program.

CONTEXT CLUES
When writers use specialized terms, they often define these terms in the text. For example, the word *biodegradable* in paragraph 4 is defined by the phrase "meaning it should break down over time."

TEKS 2B

ARGUMENT
Effective arguments address and respond to opposing points of view. However, in paragraph 5, the speaker introduces a counterargument using ad hominem. This rhetorical fallacy is based on personal attacks, such as name-calling.

TEKS 11A, 11B

EVALUATING
As a reader, you must evaluate the effectiveness of persuasive text. To do this, examine the claim and the reasoning and evidence that support it. For example, in paragraph 5 the speaker provides facts and examples to refute, or prove false, counterarguments that a recycling program is difficult and expensive to implement.

TEKS 11A; Fig. 19B

GO ON

Name ______________________________ Date ______________

6 A further effect of a school-supported paper-recycling program would be to show that we, as students, are responsible and thoughtful. A recent survey that appeared in the school newspaper revealed that 58 percent of adults see teenagers as people who are mostly interested in dating and shopping. We are interested in these things, but we also understand the importance of issues like recycling. We know that what we do now affects the world we live in tomorrow. If we were not concerned about the future, we would not have organized a carnival last year to raise money for endangered whales. Young people care as much about serious issues as adults do.

7 Of course, we should not and cannot stop using paper. What we should do is "think outside the box" and figure out a way to reuse our valuable resources. A recycling program is an inexpensive and easy way to help us accomplish a goal that we all want.

ARGUMENT
The speaker restates her position in the conclusion. Notice the overgeneralization she makes in the last sentence and consider the author's purpose in making it.

TEKS 11A, 11B; Fig. 19B

GO ON

Name ______________________________ Date ______________

Use "One Hundred Trees, Please" (pp. 37–39) to answer questions 1–7.

1 In paragraph 2, the speaker supports her argument to start a paper recycling program with the reasoning that —

A paper is a necessary resource for schools that will run out if action is not taken

B students throw out too many sheets of paper without using the back

C paper is a product of wood and is very inexpensive to make

D students use a lot of paper, and recycling it will protect the environment

EXPLANATION: Determine how the evidence in the paragraph relates to the speaker's position. **D** is correct because this answer most accurately summarizes the speaker's reasoning.

- **A** is incorrect because the speaker does not suggest that recycling will prevent a paper shortage.
- **B** is incorrect because the speaker makes no references to whether students use the front and back of sheets of paper.
- **C** is incorrect because these facts do not directly support the speaker's argument for starting a recycling program.

TEKS 11A; Fig. 19E

2 In the last sentence of paragraph 2, the phrase "before it's too late to save it" appeals to listeners' sense of —

F joy

G anger

H fear

J pity

EXPLANATION: Rather than relying on facts or logic, emotional appeals try to influence the audience's feelings. **H** is correct because the speaker appeals to listeners' fear that failing to take action will have drastic consequences.

- **F** is incorrect because people would not be joyous about irreversible damage to the planet.
- **G** and **J** are incorrect. Anger or pity would not be the typical emotional reactions to concerns about saving the planet.

TEKS 11A; Fig. 19D

GO ON

Name ______________________ Date ______________

3 Which of the following correctly identifies the rhetorical fallacy in paragraph 3?

A The speaker exaggerates the amount of forested land that existed in prehistoric times.

B The speaker asserts that anyone who doubts that humans are responsible for the loss of forests is crazy.

C The speaker falsely concludes that one hundred trees is nearly equivalent to an entire forest.

D The speaker suggests that trees help people breathe easier because they produce oxygen.

EXPLANATION: In persuasive texts, evidence must be provided to support all conclusions. Merely insulting people who disagree is a way of distracting readers from a lack of evidence or solid reasoning. **B** is correct. The speaker uses name-calling, an ad hominem fallacy, instead of supporting her conclusion about what caused the decrease in trees.

- **A** is incorrect. The speaker presents the amount of forested land in prehistoric times as a scientific estimate.
- **C** is incorrect because a forest is defined as a large area of land with many trees.
- **D** is incorrect. It is a fact that trees produce oxygen that people breathe.

TEKS 11B; Fig. 19B

4 By quoting the published author Marjorie Lamb in paragraph 5, the writer —

F strengthens her argument through an appeal to authority

G weakens her argument by relying on outside sources

H makes a personal attack on her audience

J provides an example of cause-and-effect reasoning

EXPLANATION: As the author of a published book on the environment, Lamb has a certain amount of authority. Finding quotations from authorities that support your argument is an effective persuasive technique. **F** is correct.

- **G** is incorrect. As long as the "outside source" is reputable and supports the argument, it strengthens rather than weakens it.
- **H** is incorrect. Although the writer does begin the paragraph with an ad hominem attack, her reference to Lamb is not an attack in itself.
- **J** is incorrect. An appeal to authority is not the same as cause-and-effect reasoning, although it can support such reasoning.

TEKS 11A; Fig. 19B

5 What does the word revealed mean in paragraph 6?

A Showed

B Misled

C Obscured

D Suggested

EXPLANATION: The context clue "appeared" makes it clear that the survey was published in the school newspaper, and the speaker is citing the results. **A** is correct. The survey showed how adults view teenagers' interests.

- **B** and **C** are incorrect. The context does not suggest that the survey was misleading.
- **D** is incorrect. The purpose of a survey is to collect responses, not to make suggestions.

TEKS 2B

GO ON

Name ____ Date ____________________

6 In paragraph 6, the speaker overgeneralizes when she suggests that —

F the recent carnival at the school shows that the recycling program will be successful

G recycling paper will help raise money for endangered animals

H 58 percent of adults think teens are most concerned about dating and shopping

J all young people care about serious issues because students at her school raised money for endangered animals

EXPLANATION: An overgeneralization is a broad conclusion drawn from a small amount of factual information. In paragraph 6, the speaker draws the conclusion that all teens are concerned about serious issues because some students at her school held a fundraiser for endangered whales. **J** is correct.

- **F** and **G** are incorrect. The speaker uses the fundraiser for endangered whales as an example of how students have shown their concern for the future. The fundraiser is not directly related to the recycling program.
- **H** is incorrect. The survey results are factual information from the school newspaper and not an overgeneralization made by the speaker.

TEKS 11B; Fig. 19B

7 Which of the following statements offers the best overall evaluation of the speaker's argument?

A The argument is very effective but lacks an introduction and a conclusion.

B The argument is mostly effective but weakened by some unsound reasoning.

C The argument is somewhat ineffective because it fails to include evidence that relates to the position.

D The argument is ineffective because all evidence is based on unsound reasoning.

EXPLANATION: Review the speaker's claim and the reasoning and evidence used to support it. **B** is correct because although the argument contains some rhetorical fallacies, the speaker also provides sound evidence that clearly supports her position.

- **A** is incorrect because the text contains a clear introduction and conclusion.
- **C** is incorrect. All evidence clearly relates to the position.
- **D** is incorrect. The argument contains some unsound reasoning, but most of the evidence is supported by facts and examples.

TEKS 11A, 11B; Fig. 19B

STOP

Reading Literary and Informational Text: Paired Selections

In this part of the book, you will read two selections: an informational piece with instruction about the elements of expository writing and a poem with instruction about the structure and elements of poetry. Following the selections are sample questions and answers about the two pieces. The purpose of this section is to show you how to understand and analyze selections from two different genres and how to compare and contrast them.

To begin, review the TEKS that relate to expository texts and poetry:

EXPOSITORY TEXT TEKS	WHAT IT MEANS TO YOU
(10) Comprehension of Informational Text/Expository Text Students analyze, make inferences and draw conclusions about expository text and provide evidence from text to support their understanding. Students are expected to:	
(A) evaluate a summary of the original text for accuracy of the main ideas, supporting details, and overall meaning;	You will analyze the summary of a text to see how accurate it is in capturing the text's main idea, meaning, and important details.
(B) distinguish factual claims from commonplace assertions and opinions;	You will tell the difference between statements of fact and opinions or assumptions.
(C) use different organizational patterns as guides for summarizing and forming an overview of different kinds of expository text; and	You will use different types of organization to create summaries and overviews of a text.
(D) synthesize and make logical connections between ideas within a text and across two or three texts representing similar or different genres, and support those findings with textual evidence.	You will make connections between multiple ideas found in one text or similar ideas found in different kinds of texts and support those connections with evidence.

POETRY TEKS	WHAT IT MEANS TO YOU
(4) Comprehension of Literary Text/Poetry Students understand, make inferences and draw conclusions about the structure and elements of poetry and provide evidence from text to support their understanding. Students are expected to analyze the importance of graphical elements (e.g., capital letters, line length, word position) on the meaning of a poem.	You will analyze the ways in which poems are put together and use examples from the poem to explain your analysis. You will analyze how the visual elements of a poem affect the poem's meaning.

The selections that follow provide instruction in the informational/expository text TEKS, the poetry TEKS, and other TEKS. They also cover reading comprehension skills, such as making connections between and across texts.

As you read the expository selection from *Immigrant Kids* and the poem "Learning English," notice how the authors use the elements described in the charts above. Notice also the similarities and differences in structure and meaning between the expository selection and the poem. The annotations in the margins will guide you as you read.

Name ______________________________ Date ______________

Guided Reading

Read the next two selections. Then answer the questions that follow.

from Immigrant Kids

by Russell Freedman

The following selection is part of a book about the experiences of children who left their home countries to immigrate, or move, to the United States about 100 years ago. The selection includes both researched facts and oral histories, accounts of what happened told by people who were there. Most immigrants from Europe first entered the United States at New York's Ellis Island, near the Statue of Liberty.

1 In the years around the turn of the century, immigration to America reached an all-time high. Between 1880 and 1920, 23 million immigrants arrived in the United States. They came mainly from the countries of Europe, especially from <u>impoverished</u> towns and villages in southern and eastern Europe. The one thing they had in common was a fervent[1] belief that in America, life would be better.

2 Most of these immigrants were poor. Somehow they managed to scrape together enough money to pay for their passage to America. Many immigrant families arrived penniless. Others had to make the journey in stages. Often the father came first, found work, and sent for his family later.

3 Immigrants usually crossed the Atlantic as steerage passengers. Reached by steep, slippery stairways, the steerage lay deep down in the hold of the ship. It was occupied by passengers paying the lowest fare.

4 Men, women, and children were packed into dark, foul-smelling compartments. They slept in narrow bunks stacked three high. They had no showers, no lounges, and no dining rooms. Food served from huge kettles was dished into dinner pails provided by the steamship company. Because steerage conditions were crowded and uncomfortable, passengers spent as much time as possible up on deck.

THEME
Notice the details the author includes in paragraphs 3–5 to show how difficult the journey was. These details help illustrate the theme of how strongly people wanted to live in America.

TEKS 3; Fig. 19D

1. **fervent:** intense or powerful.

GO ON

Name ______________________________ Date ______________

5 The voyage was an ordeal, but it was worth it. They were on their way to America.

6 The great majority of immigrants landed in New York City, at America's busiest port. They never forgot their first glimpse of the Statue of Liberty.

7 Edward Corsi, who later became United States Commissioner of Immigration, was a ten-year-old Italian immigrant when he sailed into New York harbor in 1907:

8 My first impressions of the New World will always remain etched in my memory, particularly that hazy October morning when I first saw Ellis Island. The steamer *Florida,* fourteen days out of Naples, filled to capacity with 1,600 natives of Italy, had weathered one of the worst storms in our captain's memory; and glad we were, both children and grown-ups, to leave the open sea and come at last through the Narrows into the Bay.

AUTHOR'S PURPOSE
The indented text beginning with paragraph 8 is an oral history, the words of someone who experienced an event firsthand. Think about the author's purpose for including Corsi's own words in this selection.

TEKS 9

9 My mother, my stepfather, my brother Giuseppe, and my two sisters, Liberta and Helvetia, all of us together, happy that we had come through the storm safely, clustered on the foredeck for fear of separation and looked with wonder on this miraculous land of our dreams.

10 Giuseppe and I held tightly to Stepfather's hands, while Liberta and Helvetia clung to Mother. Passengers all about us were crowding against the rail. Jabbered conversation, sharp cries, laughs and cheers—a steadily rising din filled the air. Mothers and fathers lifted up babies so that they too could see, off to the left, the Statue of Liberty. . . .

CONTEXT CLUES
If the word *din* in paragraph 10 is unfamiliar, look for clues nearby. These clues include "Jabbered conversation, sharp cries, laughs and cheers"—all noisy sounds—so a *din* is a lot of noise.

TEKS 2B

11 Finally the *Florida* veered to the left, turning northward into the Hudson River, and now the incredible buildings of lower Manhattan came very close to us.

12 The officers of the ship . . . went striding up and down the decks shouting orders and directions and driving the immigrants before them. Scowling and gesturing, they pushed and pulled the passengers, herding us into separate groups as though we were animals. A few moments later we came to our dock, and the long journey was over.

GO ON

Name ______________________________ Date ______________

13 But the journey was not yet over. Before they could be admitted to the United States, immigrants had to pass through Ellis Island, which became the nation's chief immigrant processing center in 1892. There they would be questioned and examined. Those who could not pass all the exams would be detained; some would be sent back to Europe. And so their arrival in America was filled with great anxiety. Among the immigrants, Ellis Island was known as "Heartbreak Island."

14 When their ship docked at a Hudson River pier, the immigrants had numbered identity tags pinned to their clothing. Then they were herded onto special ferryboats that carried them to Ellis Island. Officials hurried them along, shouting "Quick! Run! Hurry!" in half a dozen languages.

QUESTIONING
Pause from time to time to ask yourself questions about the selection. For example, here a reader might wonder, "How would people feel about being treated so rudely after everything they went through to get to America?"

Fig. 19B

15 Filing into an enormous inspection hall, the immigrants formed long lines separated by iron railings that made the hall look like a great maze.

16 Now the examinations began. First the immigrants were examined by two doctors of the United States Health Service. One doctor looked for physical and mental abnormalities. When a case aroused suspicion, the immigrant received a chalk mark on the right shoulder for further inspection: *L* for lameness, *H* for heart, *X* for mental defects, and so on.

17 The second doctor watched for contagious and infectious diseases. He looked especially for infections of the scalp and at the eyelids for symptoms of trachoma, a blinding disease. Since trachoma caused more than half of all medical detentions, this doctor was greatly feared. He stood directly in the immigrant's path. With a swift movement, he would grab the immigrant's eyelid, pull it up, and peer beneath it. If all was well, the immigrant was passed on.

18 Those who failed to get past both doctors had to undergo a more thorough medical exam. The others moved on to the registration clerk, who questioned them with the aid of an interpreter: What is your name? Your nationality? Your occupation? Can you read and write? Have you ever been in prison? How much money do you have with you? Where are you going?

19 Some immigrants were so flustered that they could not answer. They were allowed to sit and rest and try again.

GO ON

Name ______________________________ Date ______________

20 About one immigrant out of every five or six was detained for additional examinations or questioning.

21 The writer Angelo Pellegrini has recalled his own family's detention at Ellis Island:

22 We lived there for three days—Mother and we five children, the youngest of whom was three years old. Because of the rigorous physical examination that we had to submit to, particularly of the eyes, there was this terrible anxiety that one of us might be rejected. And if one of us was, what would the rest of the family do? My sister was indeed momentarily rejected; she had been so ill and had cried so much that her eyes were absolutely bloodshot, and Mother was told, "Well, we can't let her in." But fortunately, Mother was an indomitable spirit and finally made them understand that if her child had a few hours' rest and a little bite to eat she would be all right. In the end we did get through.

CONTEXT CLUES
If you don't know the word *rigorous* in paragraph 22, you can use context clues from earlier paragraphs to help you. The author describes severe and thorough physical examinations in paragraphs 16 and 17.

TEKS 2B

23 Most immigrants passed through Ellis Island in about one day. Carrying all their worldly possessions, they left the examination hall and waited on the dock for the ferry that would take them to Manhattan, a mile away. Some of them still faced long journeys overland before they reached their final destination. Others would head directly for the teeming[2] immigrant neighborhoods of New York City. . . .

24 Immigrants still come to America. Since World War II, more than 8 million immigrants have entered the country. While this is a small number compared to the mass migrations at the turn of the century, the United States continues to admit more immigrants than any other nation.

25 Many of today's immigrants come from countries within the Western Hemisphere, and from Asia and Africa as well as Europe. When they reach the United States, they face many of the same problems and hardships that have always confronted newcomers. And they come here for the same reason that immigrants have always come: to seek a better life for themselves and their children.

MAKING INFERENCES
Paragraph 25 compares immigrants past and present. You can add information about Ellis Island immigrants to what you may already know about modern immigrants. Making this connection, or inference, can help you understand the experiences of both groups.

TEKS 10; Fig. 19D

2. **teeming:** crowded, swarming.

GO ON

Name ______________________ Date ____________

Learning English

by Luis Alberto Ambroggio

The poem that follows includes very little punctuation. To help you understand where natural pauses would occur, think about the speaker's ideas as you read, and try to imagine someone saying these words in a conversation.

Life
to understand me
you must know Spanish
feel it in the blood of your soul.

If I speak another language
and use different words
for feelings that will always stay the same
I don't know
if I'll continue being
the same person.

POETRY
The word "Life" is alone on a line, but it is part of the sentence in lines 1–4. (The speaker in the poem is talking directly to life.) Consider why a poet would place a word on a line by itself.

TEKS 4

GO ON

Name ______________________________ Date ______________

Use the excerpt from *Immigrant Kids* (pp. 44–47) to answer questions 1–6.

1 Which of these is an antonym, or word opposite in meaning, for impoverished in paragraph 1?

A Crowded

B Hardworking

C Rich

D Small

EXPLANATION: Context clues in paragraph 2 make it clear that the word *impoverished* means "poor." **C** is correct because the opposite of "poor" is "rich."

- **A, B,** and **D** are incorrect. It is possible that the villages were empty or large or that the people who lived in them were lazy, but the selection does not provide evidence to support any of these definitions for *impoverished*. Therefore, their antonyms are incorrect answers.

TEKS 2B

2 Why does the author include long passages by Edward Corsi and Angelo Pellegrini?

F To give the views of different historians

G To break up the text

H To show how different their experiences were from one another

J To provide details from individual immigrants

EXPLANATION: The two passages serve an important function in the selection. **J** is correct because the author states that they are eyewitness accounts of experiences at Ellis Island.

- **F** is incorrect because Corsi and Pellegrini are not identified as historians.
- **G** is incorrect. While the two passages do break up the text, that is not their main purpose.
- **H** is incorrect because the two accounts describe similarly difficult experiences rather than provide a contrast.

TEKS 9, 10

GO ON

Name ______________________ Date ______________

3 In paragraph 22, the word indomitable means —

A caring
B lucky
C helpless
D strong

EXPLANATION: The mother refuses to allow the family to be sent back to their home country. Her quality of being indomitable gets the family through the inspections. **D** is correct. The clues "fortunately" and "finally" show that being indomitable is a positive quality and requires continued effort.

- **A** is incorrect. The mother is probably caring, but the passage provides no evidence that this quality is what helped the family in this situation.
- **B** is incorrect. Although "fortunately" means "luckily," the luck was that the mother had the quality of being indomitable, not that she herself was lucky.
- **C** is incorrect because the mother clearly takes charge of the situation and makes efforts to help her family pass inspection.

TEKS 2B

4 Which of the following best describes the overall organization of the selection?

F The author describes typical experiences of Ellis Island immigrants in chronological order.
G The author moves from least important to most important facts about immigration.
H The author states opinions about immigration and provides examples to support those opinions.
J The author compares and contrasts immigrant experiences past and present, with details about both.

EXPLANATION: An author may organize factual information in a variety of ways, even using a combination of two or more orders. **F** is correct. Most of the selection traces the journey of immigrants in the order in which events usually happened: leaving their towns, traveling on ships, arriving at the harbor, and passing through inspections.

- **G, H,** and **J** are incorrect because the selection is not organized by order of importance, opinion and support, or comparison and contrast.

TEKS 10C

GO ON

Name ______________________ Date ______________

5 Which of the following is the best summary of this selection?

- **A** About 100 years ago, a huge wave of immigrants made the difficult journey to America. Once they arrived, they faced tough inspections and the possibility of being sent back home. Today's immigrants share the same hope for a better life here.
- **B** Two young immigrants, Edward Corsi and Angelo Pellegrini, endured a difficult journey with the love and support of their families. Finally, they moved to New York City.
- **C** Immigrants today have the same experiences as immigrants had 100 years ago—they must make a long and difficult journey, pass unpleasant inspections, and then try to find a home in this new country.
- **D** Ellis Island was known among immigrants as "Heartbreak Island" because their hopes might be ruined if they failed inspection there. Many people were detained, and some had to return home penniless.

EXPLANATION: A summary states all of the key ideas from a selection, accurately and in the correct order. **A** is correct. The selection provides an overview of the immigration process 100 years ago and makes a connection to present-day immigrants.

- **B** and **D** are incorrect because these choices summarize parts of the excerpt but not the entire selection.
- **C** is incorrect. The excerpt says that people move to America today for the same reasons as they did 100 years ago, but it does not compare the journeys and inspections of the two different times.

TEKS 10A; Fig. 19E

6 Look at the following chart.

Immigrating to America in 1910

Step 1	Travel by ship, usually in steerage
Step 2	Arrive at Ellis Island and go through an inspection process
Step 3	Ride ferry to Manhattan
Step 4	

Which of the following is the best choice for Step 4?

- **F** Receive a chalk mark on the shoulder for further inspection
- **G** Receive an identity tag and then enter a line
- **H** Begin the search to find a place to live
- **J** Return to Europe

EXPLANATION: The chart summarizes the major steps in the immigration process, in the order in which they occurred. **H** is correct. Once immigrants passed inspection and rode the ferry to Manhattan, they either took long land journeys to their new homes or found homes in New York.

- **F** and **G** are incorrect because these choices list smaller events that happened as part of Step 2.
- **J** is incorrect because immigrants would take the ferry ride to Manhattan if they had passed inspection, not if they had to return to Europe.

TEKS 10C

GO ON

Name ______________________________ Date ______________

Use "Learning English" (p. 48) to answer questions 7–10.

7 The effect of placing the word *Life* (line 1) by itself on a line is to —

A show that nothing is more important than life

B emphasize that the speaker's native language is important in his entire life

C express the idea that only life understands the speaker

D make it clear that "Life" is a complete sentence

EXPLANATION: The poem expresses the idea that without Spanish, no one, not even life itself, can understand who the speaker is. **B** is correct.

- **A** is incorrect. Although life is important, language, not life, is the focus of this poem.
- **C** is incorrect. The speaker does not say whether life actually understands him.
- **D** is incorrect because a noun by itself cannot form a complete sentence. "Life" is part of the sentence in lines 1–4.

TEKS 4

8 The figurative language in line 4 serves to —

F emphasize how strongly the speaker feels about the Spanish language

G intentionally confuse the reader because the soul doesn't have blood

H create a vivid picture of the scene in the reader's mind

J compare a language to the blood that keeps the speaker alive

EXPLANATION: The "it" that the speaker says must be felt to understand him is the Spanish language. **F** is correct. The comparison shows how deeply the language must be felt.

- **G** is incorrect because figurative language is not used to confuse.
- **H** is incorrect because this example does not appeal to the sense of sight.
- **J** is incorrect. The speaker says that the language should be felt in the "blood of your soul," not that the language *is* the blood.

TEKS 4, 8

GO ON

Name ______________________________ Date ______________

9 Which of the following best describes the speaker's attitude toward learning English?

A He dislikes it because it is making him forget Spanish.

B He understands how useful it will be to speak English in the United States.

C He feels that it is inadequate for expressing himself.

D He finds the language too complicated and would prefer to speak only Spanish.

EXPLANATION: The speaker says that the only way to understand him is to know the Spanish language. **C** is correct.

- **A** is incorrect. The speaker provides no evidence that he could ever forget Spanish.
- **B** is incorrect. The speaker does not say why he is learning English.
- **D** is incorrect. The speaker does not express the idea that he finds English complicated.

TEKS 4; Fig. 19D

10 Which of the following best expresses the theme or message of this poem?

F Learning to speak another language is difficult.

G A person's native language is an important part of who he or she is.

H Feelings are the same, no matter what words are used to describe them.

J People change when they start speaking a different language.

EXPLANATION: The speaker doesn't know "if I'll continue being / the same person" if he uses "different words." He identifies who he is with the Spanish language. **G** is correct.

- **F** is incorrect because the speaker does not identify any difficulties in learning English.
- **H** is incorrect. Feelings do not change when described with different words, but that is not the poem's message.
- **J** is incorrect. The speaker does not imply that everyone changes when they learn a new language, only that he himself might.

TEKS 3, 4

GO ON

Name ______________________________ Date ______________

Use the excerpt from *Immigrant Kids* and "Learning English" (pp. 44–48) to answer questions 11–12.

11 What is one difference between the attitudes of Edward Corsi and the speaker in "Learning English"?

A Unlike the speaker of the poem, Corsi does not know what to expect in his new home.

B Corsi cares about his family members, unlike the speaker of the poem.

C Corsi enjoys speaking English, unlike the speaker of the poem.

D Unlike the speaker of the poem, Corsi does not worry about how his new life might change him.

EXPLANATION: The words of Corsi and the poem's speaker reflect very different attitudes. While Corsi says he "looked with wonder on this miraculous land of our dreams," the poem's speaker says, "I don't know / if I'll continue being / the same person." **D** is correct. Corsi expresses eagerness about the new life ahead of him in America, while the speaker of the poem is hesitant about how learning English may change him.

- **A** is incorrect. Both Corsi and the speaker of the poem are unsure of exactly what this new life holds for them.
- **B** is incorrect. Although the speaker of the poem does not mention his family members, there is no evidence that he does not care about them.
- **C** is incorrect. Corsi does not mention anything about learning English, although it probably would have been a new language for him.

TEKS 4, 10; Fig. 19F

12 Which statement is supported by both the excerpt and the poem?

F Some people adapt better to new situations than others do.

G Moving to a new country is an ordeal.

H Embarking on a new way of life can be challenging.

J People can express themselves accurately only in their first language.

EXPLANATION: A statement supported by both selections may be a theme or message they both share. **H** is correct. In both selections, people struggle with beginning a new way of life—moving to a new country in the excerpt and speaking a new language in the poem.

- **F** is incorrect. The people in the excerpt endure many difficulties and readily adapt to new situations. There is no evidence that the poem's speaker is having trouble adapting, only that he is thoughtfully considering what this new situation means to him.
- **G** and **J** are incorrect. G applies only to the book excerpt, and J applies only to the poem.

TEKS 3, 10D; Fig. 19F

STOP

Reading Practice

Name ________________________________ Date ________________

Reading Practice

Read this selection. Then answer the questions that follow.

What Happened During the Ice Storm

by Jim Heynen

My notes about what I am reading

In the woodlands and fields of the United States, it is not uncommon for people to hunt pheasants, which are medium-to-large game birds. Pheasants are especially good at hiding and are a challenge for hunters to find.

1 One winter there was a freezing rain. "How beautiful!" people said when things outside started to shine with ice. But the freezing rain kept coming. Tree branches glistened like glass. Then broke like glass. Ice thickened on the windows until everything outside blurred. Farmers moved their livestock into the barns, and most animals were safe. But not the pheasants. Their eyes froze shut.

2 Some farmers went ice-skating down the gravel roads with clubs to <u>harvest</u> pheasants that sat helplessly in the roadside ditches. The boys went out into the freezing rain to find pheasants too. They saw dark spots along a fence. Pheasants, all right. Five or six of them. The boys slid their feet along slowly, trying not to break the ice that covered the snow. They slid up close to the pheasants. The pheasants pulled their heads down between their wings. They couldn't tell how easy it was to see them huddled there.

3 The boys stood still in the icy rain. Their breath came out in slow puffs of steam. The pheasants' breath came out in quick little white puffs. Some of them lifted their heads and turned them from side to side, but they were blindfolded with ice and didn't flush.[1] The boys had not brought clubs, or sacks, or anything but themselves. They stood over the pheasants, turning their own heads, looking at each other, each expecting the other to do something. To pounce on a pheasant, or to yell "Bang!" Things around them were shining and dripping with icy rain. The barbed-wire fence. The fence

1. **flush:** to suddenly take flight.

GO ON

My notes about what I am reading

posts. The broken stems of grass. Even the grass seeds. The grass seeds looked like little yolks inside gelatin[2] whites. And the pheasants looked like unborn birds glazed in egg white. Ice was hardening on the boys' caps and coats. Soon they would be covered with ice too.

4 Then one of the boys said, "Shh." He was taking off his coat, the thin layer of ice splintering in flakes as he pulled his arms from the sleeves. But the inside of the coat was dry and warm. He covered two of the crouching pheasants with his coat, rounding the back of it over them like a shell. The other boys did the same. They covered all the helpless pheasants. The small gray hens and the larger brown cocks. Now the boys felt the rain soaking through their shirts and freezing. They ran across the slippery fields, unsure of their footing, the ice clinging to their skin as they made their way toward the blurry lights of the house.

2. **gelatin:** a jellylike substance.

Name ______________________________ Date ______________

Use "What Happened During the Ice Storm" (pp. 56–57) to answer questions 1–6.

1 In paragraph 2, the word <u>harvest</u> means —

A to pick vegetables
B to receive something
C to kill something
D a season of the year

2 Which of the following best describes the importance of the setting to the plot of the story?

F The freezing rain causes tree branches to break.
G Farmers can ice-skate on their way to catch pheasants.
H The freezing rain makes the pheasants helpless.
J The boys shield the pheasants with their coats.

3 From whose point of view is the story told?

A One of the boys
B A narrator outside the story
C One of the pheasants
D One of the farmers

4 From the information in paragraph 4, the reader can conclude that the boys —

F want to yell "Bang!"
G want to protect the pheasants
H do not like being cold
J slip and fall on the ice

GO ON

Name ______________________________ Date ______________

5 Which of the following images in paragraph 1 appeals to the reader's sense of hearing?

- **A** *branches glistened like glass*
- **B** *then broke like glass*
- **C** *ice thickened on the windows*
- **D** *eyes froze shut*

6 Read these sentences from paragraph 4.

> *He covered two of the crouching pheasants with his coat, rounding the back of it over them like a shell. The other boys did the same. They covered all the helpless pheasants.*

What is surprising about the way the boys respond to the pheasants?

- **F** The narrator says that the boys are supposed to be helping the farmers kill the pheasants.
- **G** The boys might get sick without jackets or get into trouble for leaving them.
- **H** The boys were planning to rescue the pheasants and take them home.
- **J** Before this moment in the story, it is unclear what the boys will do.

STOP

Name ____________________ Date ____________

Reading Practice

Read this selection. Then answer the questions that follow.

I Was Not Alone

from I Dream a World *by Brian Lanker*

My notes about what I am reading

On December 1, 1955, Rosa Parks boarded a bus after a long workday tailoring men's clothing at a Montgomery, Alabama, department store. When the white section of the bus filled, she was arrested for refusing to give up her seat for a white passenger. Her courageous act challenged segregation, or the separation of races, a practice that became widespread in the late 1800s after slavery ended. Following Parks's arrest, African Americans refused to ride city buses until segregation on public transportation was outlawed more than a year later. Three decades after these events, Rosa Parks participated in this interview for a book about African American women who changed America.

1 As far back as I can remember, being black in Montgomery we were well aware of the inequality of our way of life. I hated it all the time. I didn't feel that, in order to have some freedom, I should have to leave one part of the United States and go to another part of the same country just because one was South and one was North.

2 My mother believed in freedom and equality even though we didn't know it for reality during our life in Alabama.

3 In some stores, if a woman wanted to go in to try a hat, they wouldn't be permitted to try it on unless they knew they were going to buy it, or they put a bag on the inside of it. In the shoe stores they had this long row of seats, and all of those in the front could be vacant, but if one of us would go in to buy, they'd always take you to the last one, to the back of the store. There were no black salespersons.

4 At the Montgomery Fair [the store where Parks worked] I did men's alterations. Beginning in December coming up to the Christmas holiday, the work was a bit heavy. When I left the store that evening, I was tired, but I was tired every day. I had planned to get an electric heating pad so I could

GO ON

My notes about what I am reading

put some heat to my shoulder and my back and neck. After I stepped up on the bus, I noticed this driver as the same one who had evicted me from another bus way back in 1943.

5 Just back of the whites there was a black man next to one vacant seat. So I sat down with him. A few white people boarded the bus and they found seats except this one man. That is when the bus driver looked at us and asked us to let him have those seats. After he saw we weren't moving immediately, he said, "Y'all make it light on yourselves and let me have those seats."

6 When he saw that I was still remaining in the seat, the driver said, "If you don't stand up, I'm going to call the police and have you arrested." I said, "You may do that."

7 Two policemen came and wanted to know what was the trouble. One said, "Why don't you stand up?" I said, "I don't think I should have to." At that point I asked the policemen, "Why do you push us around?" He said, "I don't know, but the law is the law and you're under arrest."

8 The decision was made by the three of us, my husband, my mother, and me, that I would go on and use my case as a test case, challenging segregation on the buses.

9 When I woke up the next morning and realized I had to go to work and it was pouring down rain, the first thing I thought about was the fact that I never would ride a segregated bus again. That was my decision for me and not necessarily for anybody else.

10 People just stayed off the buses because I was arrested, not because I asked them. If everybody else had been happy and doing well, my arrest wouldn't have made any difference at all.

11 The one thing I appreciated was the fact that when so many others, by the hundreds and by the thousands, joined in, there was a kind of lifting of a burden from me individually. I could feel that whatever my individual desires were to be free, I was not alone. There were many others who felt the same way.

My notes about what I am reading

12 The first thing that happened after the people stayed off was the black cab companies were willing to just charge bus fare instead of charging cab fare. Others who had any kind of car at all would give people rides. They had quite a transportation system set up. Mass meetings were keeping the morale up. They were singing and praying and raising money in the collection to buy gasoline or tires. . . .

13 The officials really became furious when they saw that the rain and bad weather or distance or any other problem didn't matter.

14 Many whites, even white Southerners, told me that even though it may have seemed like the blacks were being freed, they felt more free and at ease themselves. They thought that my action didn't just free blacks but them also.

15 Some have suffered much more than I did. Some have even lost their lives. I just escaped some of the physical—maybe not all—but some of the physical pain. And the pain still remains. From back as far as I can remember.

16 When people made up their minds that they wanted to be free and took action, then there was a change. But they couldn't rest on just that change. It was to continue.

17 It just doesn't seem that an older person like I am should still have to be in the struggle, but if I have to be in it then I have no choice but to keep on.

18 I've been dreaming, looking, for as far back as I had any thought, of what it should be like to be a human being. My desires were to be free as soon as I had learned that there had been slavery of human beings and that I was a descendant from them. If there was a proclamation[1] setting those who were slaves free, I thought they should be indeed free and not have any type of slavery put upon us.

1. **proclamation:** official announcement.

GO ON

Name ______________________________ Date ______________

Use "I Was Not Alone" (pp. 60–62) to answer questions 1–7.

1 Which of the following best describes why Rosa Parks shares her feelings about freedom in paragraph 1 and again in paragraph 18?

A To emphasize her main message or theme that all people deserve freedom
B To show that she has worked tirelessly to gain freedom
C To provide background information about her involvement in the struggle for freedom
D To explain why people should have the right to freedom, at least in the North

2 Which pattern of organization does Rosa Parks use to describe the events before and after her arrest?

F She discusses the events in order of importance.
G She compares and contrasts different points of view about the events.
H She describes the events in chronological order.
J She presents various problems and solutions surrounding the events.

3 Which of the following best describes the meaning of the expression "Y'all make it light on yourselves" in paragraph 5?

A Please exit the bus carefully.
B You need to move a little faster.
C Be courteous to the other passengers.
D Get up if you want to avoid trouble.

4 Read the following chart.

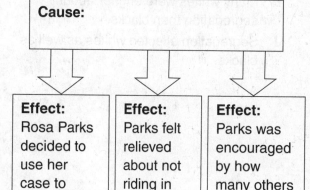

Cause:

Effect:	**Effect:**	**Effect:**
Rosa Parks decided to use her case to challenge segregation.	Parks felt relieved about not riding in another segregated bus.	Parks was encouraged by how many others decided to stay off the buses.

Which of the following belongs in the Cause box?

F Rosa Parks helped organize a local transportation system.
G Rosa Parks had to walk to work in the pouring rain.
H Rosa Parks asked people at the bus stop if they would share a cab.
J Rosa Parks was arrested for not giving up her seat on a bus.

GO ON

Name ______________________ Date ____________

5 In paragraph 12, the word <u>morale</u> means —

A donations or money
B organization and planning
C people's spirits or mood
D concern with right and wrong

6 Which of the following best summarizes Rosa Parks's main idea in paragraph 14?

F Whites and blacks thought that segregation would never be outlawed.
G Some whites and blacks disagreed with segregation.
H Many whites were angrier about segregation than blacks.
J Segregation affected whites as well as blacks.

7 Which of the following reveals how Parks's attitude about the struggle for equality evolved over time?

A She views her role in the struggle for equality as irrelevant to society today.
B She feels that she still must continue working for freedom.
C She explains why she would have done things differently.
D She remembers what happened, but the memories no longer cause her pain.

STOP

Name ______________________________ Date ______________

Reading Practice

Read this selection. Then answer the questions that follow.

The Time We Climbed Snake Mountain

by Leslie Marmon Silko

My notes about what I am reading

seeing good places
for my hands
I grab the warm parts of the cliff
and I feel the mountain as I climb.

somewhere around here
yellow spotted snake is sleeping
on his rock
in the sun.

so please
I tell them,
watch out,
don't step on yellow spotted snake,
he lives here.
The mountain is his.

GO ON

Name ______________________________ Date ____________

Use "The Time We Climbed Snake Mountain" (p. 65) to answer questions 1–3.

1 The poet's unusual arrangement of lines reflects the —

A shape of the snake as it lies curled in the sun

B movements of the speaker climbing the mountain

C breathlessness of the speaker coming down the mountain

D smoothness of the mountain's surface

2 The poet uses the snake as a symbol to convey the message that —

F snakes have many human characteristics

G snakes are a danger often faced by climbers

H there is a constant conflict between humans and nature

J nature should be protected and respected

3 Why does the poet use a capital letter at the beginning of line 14?

A All sentences in the poem begin with capital letters.

B The poet wants to place special emphasis on the idea in this sentence.

C Readers are expected to read this sentence first and work backward through the poem.

D The mountain is the most important character in the poem.

STOP

Name ______________________________ Date ______________

Reading Practice

Read this selection. Then answer the questions that follow.

from The Last Leaf

Based on a short story by O. Henry

My notes about what I am reading

CAST OF CHARACTERS

Sue

Johnsy, a nickname for **Joanna**

Eric and **Helen**, friends of Sue's

Doctor

Narrators, abbreviated as **Narr 1**, **Narr 2**, and **Narr 3**

Mr. Behrman, Sue and Johnsy's neighbor

Pharmacist

Sam, the janitor

Eric: Can you tell us just how sick Johnsy is?

Doctor: She's very, very ill—almost delirious with fever.

Helen: But it came on so suddenly, Doctor.

Doctor: Yes, that happens with pneumonia[1] sometimes. (*Putting on his coat.*) Well, I'll stop by at the pharmacist's[2] and ask him to make up some medicine. You can pick it up later, Sue.

Sue: OK, Doc. Thanks.

Helen: We'd better get home and let Johnsy have some quiet. Thanks for the party, Sue.

Eric: Let us know if there's anything we can do.

Narr 2: Sue goes into the other room, where Johnsy is lying quietly on the studio couch.

Sue: Johnsy?

1. **pneumonia:** a serious infection of the lungs.
2. **pharmacist:** someone who prepares and sells prescription medicines.

My notes about what I am reading

Narr 3: There is no sound. Sue waits a few minutes and then turns to tiptoe out. Suddenly she hears Johnsy's voice, very soft and faint.

Johnsy: Twelve. Eleven. (*Long pause.*) Ten, nine. (*Short pause.*) Eight.

Sue: What did you say, Johnsy?

Johnsy: I'm—I'm counting.

Sue: Counting what?

Johnsy: The leaves on that ivy vine. See? On the next building. You can see them in the light from the streetlamp.

Sue *(looking out)*: Oh. Yeah, I see them. They do seem to be shaking loose, what with the snow and wind. (*Looks back at Johnsy.*) So what?

Johnsy *(dreamily)*: They're dying. Falling off. Do you think I'll die too?

Sue *(really concerned but trying not to show it)*: Of course not! You're sick, but you're going to get better. I'm going out now to pick up the medicine at the pharmacist's. Just try and get some sleep, OK?

Johnsy *(very softly)*: When the last leaf falls off, perhaps I'll fall off with it. We'll go together, the leaf and I. The leaf—and my life . . . leaf . . . and life . . . (*Voice trails off.*)

Sue: That's ridiculous! Stop being so dumb!

Narr 1: Sue rushes down the stairs and out into the street, nearly colliding in the lobby with old Mr. Behrman.

Narr 2: Mr. Behrman is a painter who lives in the same building as the girls.

Narr 3: That is, he calls himself a painter. But actually he hasn't produced anything much in over forty years.

Narr 1: He's always saying that he's on the verge of painting his masterpiece.

Narr 2: But nothing ever happens. Meanwhile, he's been keeping himself alive by painting signs for small businesses.

Mr. Behrman: Hey, watch it! You want to knock an old man down?

GO ON

Name ______________________ Date ______________

My notes about what I am reading

Sue: Sorry, Mr. Behrman. But Johnsy's sick, and I've got to get some medicine for her.

Behrman: What's the matter with her?

Sue: Pneumonia, the doctor says.

Behrman *(impatiently)*: That's what happens with young people. They stay up too late; they don't dress warm; and then they get sick.

Sue: Mr. Behrman, would you do me a favor? Would you go back to our apartment and stay with Johnsy until I get back? Please?

Behrman: Well, I guess I got nothing better to do. (*Softening.*) Yes, yes. Go on.

Narr 3: Sue continues loping toward the pharmacist's, and Mr. Behrman goes upstairs. He sits down by the sleeping girl's bed and looks out the window. There are four leaves on the vine.

Narr 1: Meanwhile, Sue reaches the pharmacist's.

Pharmacist: Sue?

Sue: Yes. The medicine's for my friend, Joanna.

Pharmacist: All right, here it is. Make sure she takes a tablespoonful as soon as you get back. After that, one every four hours. Wake her up if you have to.

Sue: Thanks. I will.

Narr 2: When Sue returns home, Behrman is still sitting by the window.

Sue: Has she awakened?

Behrman: Just once. She said, "Four, three, two." I didn't know what she was talking about.

Sue: She means the leaves. She's counting the leaves on that building. Thinks when the last one falls off, she'll die.

Behrman *(looking outside)*: Better close the shade then. There's only one left. And with the snow out there and the wind coming up, it's bound to fall tonight.

Sue: You're right. (*Pulls the shade.*) You're right.

GO ON

Name ______________________________ Date ______________

My notes about what I am reading

Narr 3: Behrman goes back downstairs, and Sue catches some sleep herself after giving Johnsy her dose of medicine. When morning comes, Johnsy is already sitting up in bed, staring at the drawn shade.

Johnsy *(dully)*: Pull it up, Sue. I want to see if the last leaf has fallen.

Narr 1: Sue does as she is told. Both girls gaze out to see the last leaf still hanging from the vine.

Johnsy: I don't believe it. It couldn't still be there.

Sue: Well, you see it with your own eyes, don't you?

Johnsy: It will fall today. And I'll die.

Narr 2: All day the wind and snow rage outside. But the leaf stubbornly holds on.

Narr 3: And the next morning, when the shade is pulled up, the leaf is still there. Johnsy stares at it a long time. Then she finally speaks.

Johnsy *(slowly)*: You know, Sue, I've been thinking. Do you suppose that stubborn leaf is trying to tell me something?

Sue: Something like, "Don't be so dumb. If I can hang on, why can't you?"

Johnsy *(with a slight smile)*: Something like that, yes. Hey—do we have anything to eat around here? I mean, besides popcorn?

Sue *(happily)*: I think there's some soup. (*Hears a knock at the door.*) Just let me answer that.

Doctor *(coming in)*: How's our patient today? (*Goes into Johnsy's room.*)

Sue: Much better.

Doctor: Yes, I can see that just from looking at her. I wish I could say the same about Mr. Behrman downstairs.

Sue: Why, what's wrong with him?

GO ON

Name ______________________________ Date ______________

My notes about what I am reading

Doctor: Pneumonia too, I'm afraid. Only he's past the point of getting better. I'm taking him to the hospital now so that he can be a little more comfortable. But there's really no hope.

Narr 1: Two days pass, during which Johnsy grows stronger. On the third day she's even feeling well enough to wobble to the door when she hears a knock.

Sam, the Janitor: Hello there, Johnsy. Feeling better?

Johnsy: Yes, I am, Sam. What can I do for you?

Sam: Well, I've got some bad news, I'm afraid. Mr. Behrman died this morning.

Johnsy: Oh, no. Poor guy.

Sam: But there's something else. The doctor told me that you girls might be able to figure it out, since you knew the old guy.

Sue: What is it?

Sam: Well, I found him when he first took sick. And I thought it was funny at the time. His shoes and clothes were wet clear through, and icy cold. I couldn't understand why he'd been out so long on such a freezing night.

Sue: Neither can I.

Sam: Well, later on I found a lantern, still lighted, and a ladder that had been dragged from its place. And under some bushes I found some paints—green and yellow paints—and some brushes.

Johnsy: But what—

Sue *(suddenly understanding)*: Don't you see, Johnsy? Don't you understand now why that last leaf never fluttered or moved, even when the wind and snow beat down on it?

Johnsy *(softly)*: It was Mr. Behrman's masterpiece. The leaf he painted on the wall the night the last leaf fell.

GO ON

Name ______________________________ Date ______________

Use "The Last Leaf" (pp. 67–71) to answer questions 1–8.

1 What main purpose do the three narrators in the play serve?

- **A** They express what the characters are thinking but not saying.
- **B** They give their opinions about the events happening in the play.
- **C** They summarize what the characters are saying.
- **D** They describe the characters' actions for the audience.

2 Which of the following best describes Sue's character?

- **F** Insulting and rude
- **G** Responsible and caring
- **H** Thoughtless and silly
- **J** Serious and grouchy

3 Why is it important for Johnsy not to see the last leaf fall?

- **A** She believes that when it falls, she will die.
- **B** She wants to see Mr. Behrman's masterpiece.
- **C** She might refuse to take her medicine.
- **D** Sue doesn't want her to be saddened by the emptiness of winter.

4 Which lines provide the best context clue for the word colliding in line 39?

- **F** Lines 40–41
- **G** Lines 44–45
- **H** Lines 48–49
- **J** Lines 50–51

5 What do the stage directions in lines 54 and 61 tell you about how Mr. Behrman's attitude changes?

- **A** First he is irritated by young people's carelessness, but then he shows kindness about Johnsy's illness.
- **B** First he is in a hurry, but then he suddenly realizes that he has time to help after all.
- **C** First he shows his understanding of young people, but then he becomes sad and depressed.
- **D** First he is calm and relaxed, but then he becomes tense and worried about Johnsy.

GO ON

Name ________________________________ Date ______________

6 What information do you learn from the lines of dialogue spoken by Sam the janitor, starting with line 121?

F The technique Mr. Behrman used to paint the leaf
G How Mr. Behrman caught pneumonia
H Why the leaf is Mr. Behrman's masterpiece
J What Sam was doing outside on such a cold night

7 The dialogue and stage directions in lines 140–144 make clear —

A why the leaf was attached to the vine so strongly
B why Mr. Behrman chose to do something so dangerous
C how confused Sue, Johnsy, and Sam are by what has happened
D how moved Sue and Johnsy are by Mr. Behrman's sacrifice

8 Read the diagram of events from the play.

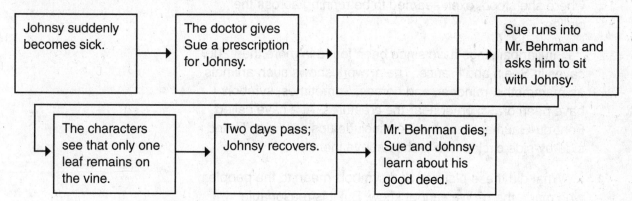

- Johnsy suddenly becomes sick. →
- The doctor gives Sue a prescription for Johnsy. →
- [empty box] →
- Sue runs into Mr. Behrman and asks him to sit with Johnsy. →
- The characters see that only one leaf remains on the vine. →
- Two days pass; Johnsy recovers. →
- Mr. Behrman dies; Sue and Johnsy learn about his good deed.

Which of the following belongs in the empty box?

F Eric and Helen leave so that Johnsy can rest.
G Mr. Behrman secretly paints a leaf on the side of the building.
H Johnsy says that when the last leaf falls from the vine, she will die.
J Sam the janitor comes to visit Sue and see how Johnsy is feeling.

Name ________________________________ Date ________________

Reading Practice

Read this selection. Then answer the questions that follow.

Making It Up As We Go: The History of Storytelling

My notes about what I am reading

by Jennifer Kroll

1 On an autumn day in 1879, eight-year-old Maria Sanz de Sautuola explored a cave on her family's land in Altamira, Spain. As her candle lit up a large chamber, Maria was startled and called to her father. "Look, Papa! Oxen!" she cried. The chamber was filled with animal paintings. From where she stood, oxen seemed to be running across the ceiling.

2 Similar paintings have since been found in more than 200 caves in Spain and France. The artwork shows such animals as mammoths, reindeer, and horses. Sometimes, symbols have been drawn on or near the creatures. At a cave called Font-du-Gaume, these symbols include upside-down *T*s and side-by-side circles with arches above them.

3 What did these pictures and symbols mean to the people who made them? We cannot know. But it is reasonable to wonder whether the images were used as a way of preserving stories—or as an aid in telling them.

STONE-AGE STORYTELLERS

4 Maria and her father, Marcelino, found stone tools, pieces of pottery, oyster shells, and animal bones nearby before uncovering the art. Marcelino figured the items, and therefore the artwork, were created by prehistoric people called Cro-Magnons. Cro-Magnons were hunters and gatherers who lived from about 40,000 to 10,000 years ago. They did not have written language as we do. But surely they had stories.

5 Imagine a Cro-Magnon storyteller standing in the Altamira cave, lighting up pictures to show parts of a story. Perhaps he stood where Maria stood. Maybe the flicker of fire from his torch made the oxen seem to run.

GO ON

Name ________________________________ Date ____________

PASS IT ON, PASS IT DOWN

My notes about what I am reading

6 Writing is a recent invention, only about 5,000 to 6,000 years old. Among the first people to develop a writing system were the Sumerians. They lived in the region that is now Iraq. Their writing system, called cuneiform, dates back to before 3000 B.C. The Sumerians wrote by pressing marks into moist clay tablets with a sharp reed. The tablets would be baked, hardening the clay so that it would last. They kept detailed business and government records. The Sumerians also wrote down stories. The *Epic of Gilgamesh* is a Sumerian story that's still told today. It was written on clay tablets that have lasted thousands of years.

7 Before developing writing, the Sumerians kept stories alive in the way most groups have throughout time. They passed on tales by word of mouth. Many of these ancient stories were written into the *Epic of Gilgamesh*. But the tales were passed from person to person for years before being pressed into clay.

8 A culture that passes on stories by word of mouth is said to have an *oral tradition*. The stories of such a culture differ from those of a *chirographic* (ky ruh GRAF ihk), or writing, culture in some ways. For one thing, written stories remain the same with each reading. But unwritten stories change with every telling. Each storyteller cannot help but give each story his or her own twist.

PREHISTORIC BLOGGERS?

9 The idea that a story may never be told the same twice might seem to go against the belief that a story is a permanent creation. Then again, maybe not. After all, we're used to seeing stories change as they shift forms—when a novel is made into a film, for example, or a film into a comic book.

10 We still pass on stories by word of mouth, just as our ancestors did. Think of campers telling scary stories around a fire or fishers swapping "biggest catch" stories. Most people like to give a story their own "spin." Think of news passed around the school cafeteria or by Internet bloggers. Most Web writers don't just tell you what happened; they tell you what they *think* about what happened. The journalists Gregory Curtis and Daniel Burnstein have (separately) suggested that the Cro-Magnons might have done something similar when they drew symbols around cave paintings. Could the symbols be comments added to a story by later viewers or tellers? It is an intriguing idea. What do you think?

GO ON

Name ______________________________ Date ________________

FROM DRAWING TO WRITING

My notes about what I am reading

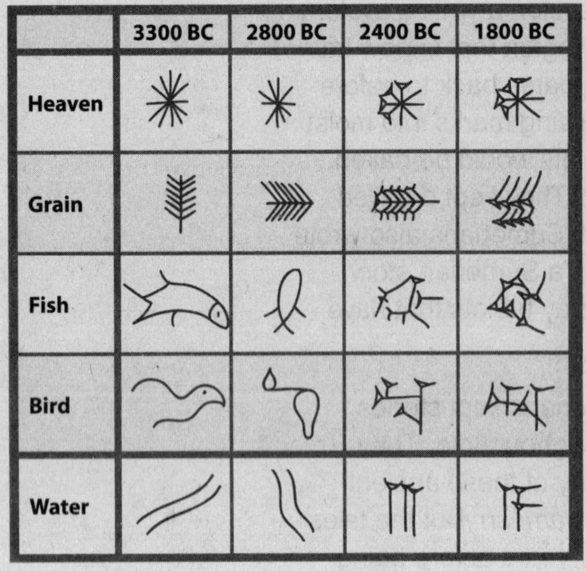

11 The Sumerians first wrote by using pictures to represent things and ideas. Gradually, the pictures became more like abstract symbols and less like illustrations of what they represented. These examples show how Sumerian writing changed over time.

THE RARE AND WONDERFUL WRITTEN WORD

12 Just how new and novel is writing? Consider these facts:

- Modern humans (*Homo sapiens*) have existed for between 100,000 and 150,000 years. The earliest written language, though, dates from only 5,000 to 6,000 years ago.
- Perhaps tens of thousands of different languages have existed in human history. Stories have been told orally in most of these languages. But ***written*** stories exist in only a small percentage of all languages—about 106!
- About 6,000 languages are spoken in the world today. Only about 78 of them have a written form that is used for recording and saving stories.
- Even today, hundreds of languages with no written form are being used all over the world.

GO ON

Name ______________________________ Date ______________

Use "Making It Up As We Go" (pp. 74–76) to answer questions 1–7.

1 How is this article organized?

A In time sequence, beginning with prehistoric times and moving forward to modern times

B By geographic area, moving from Europe to Iraq to the United States

C In categories, discussing cave paintings, the development of writing, and modern storytelling

D By comparing and contrasting ancient ways of telling stories with modern ways

2 What is the purpose of the words *STONE-AGE STORYTELLERS; PASS IT ON, PASS IT DOWN;* and *PREHISTORIC BLOGGERS*?

F Each serves as a heading to introduce the section that follows it.

G They present ideas that people disagree about for readers to consider.

H Each sums up the ideas in the text that comes before it.

J They represent the most important ideas that readers will learn from the article.

3 Which idea from the article is not supported by factual evidence?

A *The chamber was filled with animal paintings.*

B *The Sumerians wrote by pressing marks into moist clay tablets with a sharp reed.*

C *Gradually, the pictures became more like abstract symbols and less like illustrations of what they represented.*

D *Imagine a Cro-Magnon storyteller standing in the Altamira cave, lighting up pictures to show parts of a story.*

4 Which sentence from the article supports the idea that storytelling has always been important to humans?

F *The artwork shows such animals as mammoths, reindeer, and horses.*

G *Even today, hundreds of languages with no written form are being used all over the world.*

H *Before developing writing, the Sumerians kept stories alive in the way most groups have throughout time.*

J *They kept detailed business and government records.*

5 How does the graphic on page 76 help readers?

A It provides readers with an ancient story to compare to modern stories.

B It illustrates the author's point about how writing gradually changed.

C It shows the ideas that were most important to the Sumerians.

D It supports the author's statement that stories change each time they are told.

GO ON

Name ______________________ Date ______________

6 Which of the following best summarizes the article?

- **F** Maria Sanz de Sautuola made a remarkable discovery that led to the study of cave paintings all over Europe.
- **G** Storytelling dates back to prehistoric people, while writing down stories is a more recent development. Storytelling traditions continue today.
- **H** Storytellers of today owe much to the Sumerians, who first developed writing and who gave us a great work of literature, the *Epic of Gilgamesh*.
- **J** A story is never told the same way twice. People today tell stories and share their opinions in the same way that prehistoric people did long ago.

7 The author mainly wrote this article to —

- **A** teach readers about prehistoric paintings
- **B** explain that Cro-Magnons lived in caves
- **C** show how Sumerian writing changed gradually over time
- **D** suggest that the tradition of storytelling goes back to prehistoric times

STOP

Name ______________________________ Date ______________

Reading Practice

Read this selection. Then answer the questions that follow.

from The "Great Society" Speech

My notes about what I am reading

by Lyndon B. Johnson

President Lyndon B. Johnson delivered this speech before a graduating class at the University of Michigan on May 22, 1964.

1 . . . I want to talk to you today about three places where we begin to build the Great Society—in our cities, in our countryside, and in our classrooms.

2 Many of you will live to see the day, perhaps 50 years from now, when there will be 400 million Americans—four-fifths of them in urban areas. In the remainder of this century urban population will double, city land will double, and we will have to build homes, highways, and facilities equal to all those built since this country was first settled. So in the next 40 years we must rebuild the entire urban United States. . . .

3 Our society will never be great until our cities are great. Today the frontier of imagination and innovation is inside those cities and not beyond their borders.

4 New experiments are already going on. It will be the task of your generation to make the American city a place where future generations will come, not only to live but to live the good life. . . .

5 A second place where we begin to build the Great Society is in our countryside. We have always prided ourselves on being not only America the strong and America the free, but America the beautiful. Today that beauty is in danger. The water we drink, the food we eat, the very air that we breathe, are threatened with pollution. Our parks are overcrowded, our seashores overburdened. Green fields and dense forests are disappearing.

From *Public Papers of the Presidents of the United States: Lyndon B. Johnson,* 1963–64. Volume I, entry 357, pp. 704–707. Washington, D.C.: Government Printing Office, 1965.

GO ON

Name ______________________________ Date ______________

My notes about what I am reading

6 A few years ago we were greatly concerned about the "Ugly American." Today we must act to prevent an ugly America.

7 For once the battle is lost, once our natural splendor is destroyed, it can never be recaptured. And once man can no longer walk with beauty or wonder at nature his spirit will wither and his sustenance be wasted.[1]

8 A third place to build the Great Society is in the classrooms of America. There your children's lives will be shaped. Our society will not be great until every young mind is set free to scan the farthest reaches of thought and imagination. We are still far from that goal. . . .

9 In many places, classrooms are overcrowded and curricula[2] are outdated. Most of our qualified teachers are underpaid, and many of our paid teachers are unqualified. So we must give every child a place to sit and a teacher to learn from. Poverty must not be a bar to learning, and learning must offer an escape from poverty.

10 But more classrooms and more teachers are not enough. We must seek an educational system which grows in excellence as it grows in size. This means better training for our teachers. It means preparing youth to enjoy their hours of leisure as well as their hours of labor. It means exploring new techniques of teaching, to find new ways to stimulate the love of learning and the capacity for creation.

11 These are three of the central issues of the Great Society. While our Government has many programs directed at those issues, I do not pretend that we have the full answer to those problems.

12 But I do promise this: We are going to assemble the best thought and the broadest knowledge from all over the world to find those answers for America. I intend to establish working groups to prepare a series of White House conferences and meetings—on the cities, on natural beauty, on the quality of education, and on other emerging challenges. And from these meetings and from this inspiration and from these studies we will begin to set our course toward the Great Society. . . .

1. **his spirit . . . be wasted:** his spirit will shrivel and his nourishment will disappear.
2. **curricula:** programs of study.

GO ON

Name ______________________________ Date ______________

My notes about what I am reading

13 For better or for worse, your generation has been appointed by history to deal with those problems and to lead America toward a new age. You have the chance never before afforded to any people in any age. You can help build a society where the demands of morality,[3] and the needs of the spirit, can be realized in the life of the Nation.

14 So, will you join in the battle to give every citizen the full equality which God enjoins and the law requires, whatever his belief, or race, or the color of his skin?

15 Will you join in the battle to give every citizen an escape from the crushing weight of poverty?

16 Will you join in the battle to make it possible for all nations to live in enduring peace—as neighbors and not as mortal enemies?

17 Will you join in the battle to build the Great Society, to prove that our material progress is only the foundation on which we will build a richer life of mind and spirit?

18 There are those timid souls who say this battle cannot be won; that we are condemned to a soulless[4] wealth. I do not agree. We have the power to shape the civilization that we want. But we need your will, your labor, your hearts, if we are to build that kind of society.

19 Those who came to this land sought to build more than just a new country. They sought a new world. So I have come here today to your campus to say that you can make their vision our reality. So let us from this moment begin our work so that in the future men will look back and say: It was then, after a long and weary way, that man turned the exploits[5] of his genius to the full enrichment of his life.

3. **morality:** doing what is good and right.
4. **soulless:** lacking in conscience.
5. **exploits:** brilliant or daring achievements.

GO ON

Name ______________________________ Date ______________

Use the excerpt from President Johnson's "Great Society" Speech (pp. 79–81) to answer questions 1–7.

1 Which phrase from paragraph 7 provides the best context clue for splendor?

- **A** *battle is lost*
- **B** *never be recaptured*
- **C** *walk with beauty*
- **D** *spirit will wither*

2 Which statement best describes the structure of President Johnson's argument?

- **F** He discusses the causes of pollution and their effects.
- **G** He develops a comparison between the present generation and the early settlers who also had to build a nation.
- **H** He traces the great accomplishments of the United States throughout its history.
- **J** He describes the problems of the current society and ideas for the solution.

3 The president most likely delivered this speech to an audience of graduating college students because he —

- **A** needed their votes
- **B** saw them as the ones responsible for shaping the future
- **C** knew that they would be attentive and polite
- **D** thought they should be more serious about their education

4 Which of the following claims can be supported with facts and statistics?

- **F** *In the remainder of this century urban population will double, city land will double . . .*
- **G** *Our society will never be great until our cities are great.*
- **H** *We must act to prevent an ugly America.*
- **J** *And once man can no longer . . . wonder at nature his spirit will wither.*

GO ON

Name ______________________ Date ______________

5 The president's main purpose in this speech is to —

A reaffirm the importance of working for equality and civil rights

B teach Americans that there is no limit to what they can accomplish if they work together

C warn about the dangers of overcrowded cities and poor schools

D persuade Americans to support his effort to resolve the major issues confronting the nation

6 In paragraph 18, describing those people who might oppose the president's plan as *timid* is a form of —

F exaggeration

G ad hominem attack

H avoiding the issue

J stereotyping

7 Read these sentences from paragraph 5.

> *Today that beauty is in danger. The water we drink, the food we eat, the very air that we breathe, are threatened with pollution. Our parks are overcrowded, our seashores overburdened.*

What type of evidence does the president use to support his claim in this paragraph?

A Statistics

B Anecdotes

C Facts

D Examples

STOP

Name ______________________________ Date ______________

Reading Practice

Read the next two selections. Then answer the questions that follow.

Teach Your Dog the Name Game

My notes about what I am reading

by Liz Palika

1 Training your dog tends to take a serious tone; after all, much of it involves teaching your dog its place in the family, and self-control. Your dog needs to learn that it's not allowed to jump on the sofa and that it has to keep its nose out of the kitchen trashcan. That can be serious stuff.

2 However, training also can be fun. Games and tricks can challenge your skills and your dog's ability to learn. Once you have taught your dog, you can show off its tricks and amuse your friends and family. I use trick training with my therapy dogs.[1] A silly trick can help the person we're visiting laugh.

3 The name game is one of my favorites and a great way to make your dog think. Don't doubt for a minute that your dog can learn the names of many different items and people. This is a rewarding game for your dog and can come in handy around the house. Tell your dog to find your keys or your shoes. Send your dog after the remote control to the television set or to find your husband, wife, or child.

4 I have taught my dogs to identify and find many different items. If my husband calls to me from a different room and asks for something, I can hand it to my dog Dax and tell her, "Go find Paul!" It saves me from interrupting what I'm doing and gives Dax a job. She always gets praised for doing it and loves being useful.

5 I have also taught my dog Ursa to find turtles. I rescue turtles and tortoises and rehabilitate abandoned, injured or ill ones. Occasionally when I go to feed and care for the turtles, one is missing, so I tell Ursa to find it and she does. A couple of times she has even found buried turtle eggs when I didn't know any had been laid.

6 Start teaching your dog the name game by selecting two very different items, perhaps a tennis ball and a bowl. Sit on

1. **therapy dogs:** dogs trained to comfort people in difficult or stressful situations.

GO ON

My notes about what I am reading

the floor with your dog and the items and have some treats it likes. Ask it, "Where's the ball?" and bounce the ball so your dog pays attention to it or perhaps tries to grab it. When your dog touches it, say, "Good boy to find the ball!" and give it a treat.

7 When your dog responds to the ball, lay it on the floor next to the bowl and ask your dog, "Where's the ball?" Praise and reward if it gets the ball.

8 Now set something else out with the bowl and ball. Again ask, "Where's the ball?" When the dog brings it back, praise and reward it. When your dog does that well, place one of its other toys there and send the dog for the ball. If it goes for the other toy, take it away with no comment, and send the dog after the ball again. This is a critical step in the learning process, and you may need to repeat it several times. If your dog continues to go to its other toy, take it away and practice again with the original items. After a few successes, stop the training and let your dog relax. Later try again with the original items, and when your dog does it right, place its toy there again.

9 When your dog will pick up its ball from among several items, including other toys, start hiding the ball. Make it simple to start, maybe partially hidden under a magazine. As your dog's skill improves, start making the game more challenging. Hide the ball behind a chair or in another room, again only partially hidden.

10 Later, when your dog has mastered the search, have someone else hide the ball so it can't follow your scent trail to it.

11 When your dog succeeds, use the same process to teach it the names of other items. The next three items will be easier to teach. Your dog needs to understand the concept you are trying to teach: Different items have different names. Once it understands that each has a different sound or name, it will learn much faster.

12 Keep training sessions short and upbeat. With some dogs, three minutes may be too much. Other dogs may be able to concentrate for six or seven minutes. You need to know your dog and always stop before it loses interest.

13 Also, always stop with a success. If your dog is having trouble, have it do a trick you know it can do and then praise it lavishly before you stop the training session.

GO ON

Name ______________________________ Date ______________

Moco Limping

by David Nava Monreal

My notes about what I am reading

My dog hobbles
with a stick
of a leg that
he drags behind
him as he moves.
And I was a man
that wanted a
beautiful, noble
animal as a pet.
I wanted him
to be strong and
capture all the
attention by
the savage grace
of his gait.
I wanted him to
be the first
dog howling in
the pack.
The leader,
the brutal hunter
that broke through
the woods with
thunder.
But, instead
he's this rickety
little canine
that leaves trails
in the dirt
with his club foot.
He's the stumbler
that trips while
chasing lethargic[1]
bees and butterflies.

1. **lethargic:** slow and lacking energy.

GO ON

Name ______________________________ Date ______________

My notes about what I am reading

It hurts me to
see him so
abnormal,
so clumsy and
stupid.
My vain heart weeps
knowing he
is mine.
But then he turns
my way and
looks at me with
eyes that cry out
with life.
He jumps at me with
his feeble paws.
I feel his warm fur
and his imperfection is forgotten.

GO ON

Name ______________________ Date ______________

Use "Teach Your Dog the Name Game" (pp. 84–85) to answer questions 1–7.

1 The author's attitude toward the reader can best be described as —

A bossy
B friendly
C formal
D lazy

2 Look at the following chart.

Teaching a Dog the Name Game

Step 1	Place two different items on the floor near the dog.
Step 2	
Step 3	Reward or praise the dog when it touches the correct item.
Step 4	Add other items to the first two.
Step 5	
Step 6	Keep practicing.
Step 7	Hide the items you name in various places.
Step 8	
Step 9	Have someone else hide the item.
Step 10	

Choose the instruction that belongs with Steps 2, 5, 8, and 10.

F Tell the dog to get the item you name.
G Take away other items if they are distracting.
H Draw your dog's attention to the chosen item.
J Teach your dog the names of other things.

3 Which statement from the article expresses an opinion, which cannot be proved true or false?

A *I use trick training with my therapy dogs.*
B *[Dax] loves being useful.*
C *[Ursa] has even found buried turtle eggs. . . .*
D *With some dogs, three minutes may be too much.*

4 In paragraph 6, the word <u>rehabilitate</u> means to —

F rescue from danger
G sell to a collector
H take in as a pet
J return to health

GO ON

Name ______________________________ Date ______________

5 If your dog does not choose the item you name, what should you do?

A Give up because your dog cannot learn this trick.
B Keep trying, using the same procedure.
C Take away an item that may be distracting the dog.
D Praise your dog and give it a treat.

6 To have your dog practice finding a shoe, what should you do?

F Hide the shoe partway under a chair.
G Leave the shoe outside at the door.
H Put the shoe in a closet and close the door.
J Place the dog's favorite toy inside the shoe.

7 The author most likely wrote this article to —

A entertain readers with stories about dogs
B persuade readers of the importance of training dogs
C reflect on what makes dogs good companions
D inform readers about a way to train dogs

GO ON

Name ______________________ Date ______________

Use "Moco Limping" (pp. 86–87) to answer questions 8–12.

8 In lines 1–5, the poet uses figurative language to —

F create a vivid picture of how the dog walks

G explain how the dog was injured

H build a strong, repetitive rhythm that continues through the poem

J show how fit and active the dog is

9 Which statement best expresses the speaker's attitude about his ideal dog and the dog he has?

A The speaker's real dog is exactly the dog he imagined owning.

B The speaker's ideal dog is strong and powerful, while his real dog is clumsy but lovable.

C The speaker dislikes his real dog because it is embarrassing; his ideal dog would make him proud.

D The speaker's ideal dog is too brutal and howling; he would rather have a helpless dog that needs him.

10 The imagery in lines 31–34 shows that the speaker views Moco as —

F quick and entertaining

G shamefully stupid

H clumsy even at easy tasks

J a beautiful, noble pet

11 Why is line 51 longer than any other line in the poem?

A Because it contains the poem's most important idea

B To retain the poem's rhythm

C Because the poet forgot to put "is forgotten" on a separate line

D To create a pattern of rhymes at the ends of lines

12 Which statement best expresses the theme or message of this poem?

F High expectations are always rewarded.

G Love is more important than perfection.

H Pets reflect who we are.

J Life is full of disappointments.

GO ON

Name ______________________________ Date ________________

Use "Teach Your Dog the Name Game" and "Moco Limping" (pp. 84–87) to answer questions 13–15.

13 Which statement best describes the difference between the dogs in the article and the dog in the poem?

- **A** The dogs in the article enjoy playing with toys, while the dog in the poem prefers to chase insects.
- **B** The dogs in the article need to be trained, but the dog in the poem is already well trained.
- **C** The dogs in the article are smart, helpful, and capable, while the dog in the poem can do little except show his devotion to his owner.
- **D** The dogs in the article are unable to concentrate for very long, but the dog in the poem can focus because he moves more slowly.

14 The author of "Teach Your Dog the Name Game" and the speaker in "Moco Limping" both —

- **F** wish their dogs could be better
- **G** recognize their dogs' good qualities as well as their flaws
- **H** expect it to be easy to get their dogs to do what they want
- **J** consider it important to praise their dogs

15 With which of these statements would the authors of the two selections most likely agree?

- **A** It is important to be serious in all interactions with your dog.
- **B** Dogs enjoy showing off and helping humans.
- **C** All dogs can do impressive things once they are trained correctly.
- **D** Appreciate and work with the dog you have instead of expecting perfection.

STOP

Written Composition

Name ______________________________ Date ______________

Written Composition: Personal Narrative 1

READ

Some decisions are easy, like deciding to have pepperoni pizza because it's your favorite. Others are difficult because there are good points on both sides. In some cases, your decision could lead to unpleasant consequences—for you or for others.

THINK

Think back to a difficult decision you had to make. Why was it difficult? Were other people affected by your decision? What happened as a result?

WRITE

Write a personal narrative about a time when you made a difficult decision.

As you write your composition, remember to —

- ☐ focus on a controlling idea about a time when you made a difficult decision
- ☐ organize your ideas in an order that makes sense and connect ideas using transitions
- ☐ develop your ideas fully and thoughtfully, including the significance of your decision as well as its consequences
- ☐ make sure your composition is no longer than one page

TEKS 14A, 14B, 14C, 14D, 16, 19, 21

ANALYZE THE PROMPT

The prompt asks you to write a personal narrative. That means you should write about your own experience. You should not write a made-up story or tell about something that happened to someone else.

RESPOND TO THE PROMPT

- **Plan** by jotting down difficult decisions you have made. Choose the one you can most clearly explain. List key ideas about your chosen decision.
- **Draft** your response by describing events in a clear order. Include the context in which you made the decision and why it was important.
- **Revise** to use more precise wording, to vary the lengths and types of sentences you use, and to add transitions connecting ideas.
- **Edit** your writing to make sure errors won't keep the reader from understanding what you have to say.

Name ______________________ Date ______________

Benchmark Composition: Personal Narrative 1

Score Point 4

Choosing Harmony

Last summer, I was so excited to go to Girls Rock Camp. I begged my best friend, Monica, to sign up. She would play drums and I would play keyboards. It was expensive, but her mom agreed. I learned so much at camp—how to play my instrument, set up gear, write a song, promote a band, and get along with other musicians. That last part was the hardest.

ORGANIZATION/ PROGRESSION
The writer provides background information and then builds to the controlling idea of the narrative. The last sentence of the paragraph hints at a decision she will have to make.

Monica and I formed a band with talented twins, Abigail and Alice. One day, Alice shared a new song with us. Abigail and I jumped in, while Monica's drums thudded, off-rhythm. Monica was loyal, fun, sweet . . . and a terrible drummer.

Monica headed to a drum lesson. I walked her to the studio, where we waited for another lesson to end. The girl playing was amazing! She came out and Monica went in.

"Wow, you're good," I told the girl. "What's your name?"

"Latrice. What's yours?" I told her my name and my band's name. "I've heard you!" she said. "Wish I was in that band."

What was I going to do? Should I kick out my best friend so our band could have a chance to be great? I worried and avoided Monica for days. Abigail and Alice deserved a good drummer. They could be stars, but what was I going to be?

ORGANIZATION/ PROGRESSION
The writer clearly states the controlling idea—the decision on which the narrative focuses.

Finally I couldn't stand it. I told Abigail and Alice that Latrice wanted to be in their band and that I needed to quit. Maybe Monica and I could start a different band just for fun. I expected to feel like I'd thrown away a winning lottery ticket, but I felt light and free instead—the opposite of how Monica looked arriving for practice, lugging her drums.

DEVELOPMENT OF IDEAS
The writer uses a striking comparison to show how she thought she would feel about her decision.

"I hate playing drums!" she huffed. The three of us held our breath. "I'm sorry. I hate hauling these things. I want to play violin instead. Please don't be mad."

Right then, Latrice peeked in. "Is this a bad time?"

Even if our band, The 5 of Us, hadn't won the end-of-camp contest (thanks to Monica's violin playing!), I would have been happy. In fact, even if the other girls had decided not to play with Monica and me, I'd have been happy. My decision wasn't easy, but I knew I'd rather be in the audience with my best friend than on stage without her.

DEVELOPMENT OF IDEAS
The writer emphasizes the reasons for her decision after discussing its consequences.

Name ______________________________ Date ______________

Personal Narrative 1: Score Summary and Rubric **Score Point 4**

This personal narrative successfully explores a difficult decision. The reader is given enough information to understand the factors involved in the decision and its importance. A clear chronological organization is maintained, and transitions effectively connect events. The writer has chosen words carefully to create an appropriate tone, and the writing is clear and engaging.

	ORGANIZATION/ PROGRESSION	DEVELOPMENT OF IDEAS	USE OF LANGUAGE CONVENTIONS
4	• Uses appropriate structure or form for purpose and demands of prompt; narrative strategies enhance effectiveness of writing • Uses details effectively; sustains focus, creating unity and coherence • Controls progression with transitions showing relationships among ideas	• Employs specific, well-chosen details that develop key literary elements • Engages reader through a thoughtful narrative that may approach topic from an unusual perspective; demonstrates a deep understanding of prompt	• Shows strong understanding of word choice appropriate to form, purpose, and tone • Uses purposeful, varied, and controlled sentences • Demonstrates command of conventions so that narrative is fluent and clear even if the writing contains minor errors
3	• Uses mostly effective structure or form for demands of prompt; narrative strategies generally enhance effectiveness of writing • Mostly uses details effectively; narrative is coherent though may lack overall unity • Mostly controls progression of ideas with transitions	• Employs specific details that add some substance to the narrative; details generally contribute to key literary elements • Demonstrates some depth of thought, with an original rather than formulaic approach and a good understanding of the task	• Shows basic understanding of word choice appropriate to form, purpose, and tone; diction generally succeeds in communicating meaning • Uses varied and mostly controlled sentences • Demonstrates general command of conventions; errors do not seriously affect clarity or fluency of narrative
2	• May use form or structure inappropriate to demands of the prompt; narrative strategies contribute only marginally to effectiveness • May use some details that do not contribute to narrative; focus may not be sustained • Controls progression of thought inconsistently; may lack clear links among ideas	• Fails to develop narrative beyond a minimal level because details may be inappropriate or incompletely developed; details only marginally contribute to key literary elements • Uses somewhat formulaic approach to prompt, reflecting limited understanding of task	• Shows limited understanding of word choice; may use basic or simplistic vocabulary • May use awkward, uncontrolled sentences • Demonstrates partial command of conventions, possibly with significant errors that weaken the fluency of writing
1	• Uses inappropriate form or structure • Lacks focus and apt details; coherence/unity are weak • Has weak progression of thought, with lack of meaningful transitions	• Exhibits weak development of ideas because details and examples are inappropriate, vague, or insufficient • Demonstrates lack of understanding of prompt and/or vague approach	• Lacks appropriate word choice; uses imprecise or general vocabulary • Uses simplistic, awkward, or uncontrolled sentences • Demonstrates limited or no command of conventions

Name ______________________________ Date ______________

Benchmark Composition: Personal Narrative 1

Score Point 2

My Difficult Decision

One time I had to make a really hard decision. We were trying to decide where to go on vacation and I wanted to go to Sea World but my brother wanted to go to the beach instead. I told him some really good reasons why going to Sea World would be more fun but he wouldn't change his mind. I was so mad that my mom agreed with him because the beach sounded really boring to me. We wound up going to the beach for vacation anyway. It turned out to be fun after all, though, because I got to go parasailing, wich is kind of like water sking but up in the air. That was really fun. Exept that I got sunburned. The drive to the coast took way too long, though. So that part was boring. Looking back on it now, I wonder if I would of made the same decision knowing what I know now about how fun the beach could be once we got there. We still never went to Sea World, though.

DEVELOPMENT OF IDEAS
The writer identifies the decision but does not communicate its importance or provide reasons.

USE OF LANGUAGE CONVENTIONS
The writer makes several errors in spelling, usage, and sentence structure.

Name ______________________________ Date ______________

Personal Narrative 1: Score Summary and Rubric **Score Point 2**

This narrative fails to discuss the consequences of a decision or explain why it was important. Events are mostly organized in order but some shifts in time occur. Word choices are not specific, and the writer makes numerous errors in the conventions of writing.

	ORGANIZATION/ PROGRESSION	DEVELOPMENT OF IDEAS	USE OF LANGUAGE CONVENTIONS
4	• Uses appropriate structure or form for purpose and demands of prompt; narrative strategies enhance effectiveness of writing • Uses details effectively; sustains focus, creating unity and coherence • Controls progression with transitions showing relationships among ideas	• Employs specific, well-chosen details that develop key literary elements • Engages reader through a thoughtful narrative that may approach topic from an unusual perspective; demonstrates a deep understanding of prompt	• Shows strong understanding of word choice appropriate to form, purpose, and tone • Uses purposeful, varied, and controlled sentences • Demonstrates command of conventions so that narrative is fluent and clear even if the writing contains minor errors
3	• Uses mostly effective structure or form for demands of prompt; narrative strategies generally enhance effectiveness of writing • Mostly uses details effectively; narrative is coherent though may lack overall unity • Mostly controls progression of ideas with transitions	• Employs specific details that add some substance to the narrative; details generally contribute to key literary elements • Demonstrates some depth of thought, with an original rather than formulaic approach and a good understanding of the task	• Shows basic understanding of word choice appropriate to form, purpose, and tone; diction generally succeeds in communicating meaning • Uses varied and mostly controlled sentences • Demonstrates general command of conventions; errors do not seriously affect clarity or fluency of narrative
2	• May use form or structure inappropriate to demands of the prompt; narrative strategies contribute only marginally to effectiveness • May use some details that do not contribute to narrative; focus may not be sustained • Controls progression of thought inconsistently; may lack clear links among ideas	• Fails to develop narrative beyond a minimal level because details may be inappropriate or incompletely developed; details only marginally contribute to key literary elements • Uses somewhat formulaic approach to prompt, reflecting limited understanding of task	• Shows limited understanding of word choice; may use basic or simplistic vocabulary • May use awkward, uncontrolled sentences • Demonstrates partial command of conventions, possibly with significant errors that weaken the fluency of writing
1	• Uses inappropriate form or structure • Lacks focus and apt details; coherence/unity are weak • Has weak progression of thought, with lack of meaningful transitions	• Exhibits weak development of ideas because details and examples are inappropriate, vague, or insufficient • Demonstrates lack of understanding of prompt and/ or vague approach	• Lacks appropriate word choice; uses imprecise or general vocabulary • Uses simplistic, awkward, or uncontrolled sentences • Demonstrates limited or no command of conventions

Name ______________________________ Date ____________________

Written Composition: Personal Narrative 2

READ

School is not the only place to learn things. All kinds of experiences can teach lessons about life.

THINK

Think about an experience you had that taught you something important. What was the experience, and how did it make you feel at the time? What did you learn?

WRITE

Write a personal narrative about a time when you learned an important life lesson.

As you write your composition, remember to —

- ☐ focus on a controlling idea about a time when you learned an important life lesson
- ☐ organize your narrative in a way that clearly shows the sequence of events and uses effective transitions
- ☐ develop your ideas fully and thoughtfully, including facts and details about the event as well as its importance
- ☐ make sure your composition is no longer than one page

TEKS 14B, 14C, 14D, 16, 19, 20, 21

ANALYZE THE PROMPT

The prompt asks you to write a personal narrative. This means you should write from the first-person point of view, using pronouns like *I* and *we* to describe an experience from your own life.

RESPOND TO THE PROMPT

- **Plan** by listing personal experiences from which you learned something. Select one experience that taught you an important lesson and that you can describe vividly.
- **Draft** your response by describing events in a clear order. Explain what you learned and why it was important.
- **Revise** to use more precise wording, to vary the lengths and types of sentences you use, and to add transitions connecting ideas.
- **Edit** your writing to correct any errors that could distract readers from understanding your personal story and its importance.

Name ______________________________ Date ______________

Benchmark Composition: Personal Narrative 2

Score Point 4

No Fear

Faith is trusting someone to the fullest extent. Faith is closing your eyes and trusting someone to see for you. Faith is believing in the impossible. During a recent hiking trip, I realized that when you have faith, you can overcome your fear.

ORGANIZATION/ PROGRESSION
The writer clearly establishes her focus in the introduction. Readers know she is writing about a hiking trip that taught her a lesson about faith.

Standing in Bear Canyon, one of the steepest trails in Guadalupe National Park, wind enveloped me. All I could see was wind blowing the trees until their branches touched the ground. All I could hear was the wind whistling through the air. And all I could feel inside myself was fear.

For over an hour my father and I had been descending from the mountaintop. With every step I became weaker, with every blast of wind I grew more tired, and with every stumble I became more and more discouraged. The rocks and pebbles underfoot became pieces of frustration, causing me to slip and fall. As much as I wanted to stop and rest, the wind kept pushing me like an invisible hand. Trudging forward without looking, I ran into my father, who had stopped abruptly. I soon realized why. We had come to a part of the trail where it became so steep it was almost vertical. Tears filled my eyes.

DEVELOPMENT OF IDEAS
The writer presents her narrative in a clear sequence of events. Transitions show how events and ideas are connected.

"Dad, I can't do this!" I screamed over the wind.

"Yes, you can!" he responded. He then grabbed my shoulders and looked right into my eyes. "Do you trust me?" he questioned.

DEVELOPMENT OF IDEAS
Specific details, such as dialogue, engage the reader and reveal how the writer felt during the experience.

"Y-yes," I responded, though I was still unsure. He grabbed my shaking hands and began to help me descend. His footing was so precise that I never stumbled. His grip on my hand was so firm that I soon lost all fear and began to relax. When we finally reached the bottom of the mountain, I looked into his face and said, "I trust you," and this time I meant it. I trusted him completely.

That day I learned more than just hiking. I learned to have faith. This experience has changed me forever. I now realize that there was more fear inside of me than there was danger on the trail. Because of my own fear, I learned to put trust and faith in others when I couldn't put it in myself. That is what faith is all about.

DEVELOPMENT OF IDEAS
In her conclusion, the writer shows her understanding of the prompt by emphasizing the life lesson she learned from her experience.

Name ______________________________ Date ______________

Personal Narrative 2: Score Summary and Rubric **Score Point 4**

This personal narrative successfully describes an experience that taught the writer a life lesson. Skillfully using parallel structures *(Faith is . . .)*, the writer quickly establishes her focus and then uses details and dialogue to create a coherent narrative. The writing is clear and engaging.

	ORGANIZATION/ PROGRESSION	DEVELOPMENT OF IDEAS	USE OF LANGUAGE CONVENTIONS
4	• Uses appropriate structure or form for purpose and demands of prompt; narrative strategies enhance effectiveness of writing • Uses details effectively; sustains focus, creating unity and coherence • Controls progression with transitions showing relationships among ideas	• Employs specific, well-chosen details that develop key literary elements • Engages reader through a thoughtful narrative that may approach topic from an unusual perspective; demonstrates a deep understanding of prompt	• Shows strong understanding of word choice appropriate to form, purpose, and tone • Uses purposeful, varied, and controlled sentences • Demonstrates command of conventions so that narrative is fluent and clear even if the writing contains minor errors
3	• Uses mostly effective structure or form for demands of prompt; narrative strategies generally enhance effectiveness of writing • Mostly uses details effectively; narrative is coherent though may lack overall unity • Mostly controls progression of ideas with transitions	• Employs specific details that add some substance to the narrative; details generally contribute to key literary elements • Demonstrates some depth of thought, with an original rather than formulaic approach and a good understanding of the task	• Shows basic understanding of word choice appropriate to form, purpose, and tone; diction generally succeeds in communicating meaning • Uses varied and mostly controlled sentences • Demonstrates general command of conventions; errors do not seriously affect clarity or fluency of narrative
2	• May use form or structure inappropriate to demands of the prompt; narrative strategies contribute only marginally to effectiveness • May use some details that do not contribute to narrative; focus may not be sustained • Controls progression of thought inconsistently; may lack clear links among ideas	• Fails to develop narrative beyond a minimal level because details may be inappropriate or incompletely developed; details only marginally contribute to key literary elements • Uses somewhat formulaic approach to prompt, reflecting limited understanding of task	• Shows limited understanding of word choice; may use basic or simplistic vocabulary • May use awkward, uncontrolled sentences • Demonstrates partial command of conventions, possibly with significant errors that weaken the fluency of writing
1	• Uses inappropriate form or structure • Lacks focus and apt details; coherence/unity are weak • Has weak progression of thought, with lack of meaningful transitions	• Exhibits weak development of ideas because details and examples are inappropriate, vague, or insufficient • Demonstrates lack of understanding of prompt and/or vague approach	• Lacks appropriate word choice; uses imprecise or general vocabulary • Uses simplistic, awkward, or uncontrolled sentences • Demonstrates limited or no command of conventions

Name ______________________________ Date ______________

Benchmark Composition: Personal Narrative 2

Score Point 2

What I Learned

One time I hurt my sister in the car, it was an accident. We always argued. We were yelling. Mom told us to stop yelling. I pushed you and you hit the door. Mom didn't see that your mouth was bloody but I saw. Your face got red and you cried but you didn't say anything. I told mom what had happened, and she had gotten so mad. She stopped the car. We went to the hospital. He said you were going to be okay. I felt completely guilty and sad for you. He said your teeth weren't going to fall out. I could see that you were still in pain and I felt so bad. The important lesson I learned is how fast you can hurt someone without trying and to slow down and be more careful in the car. I also learned to be more careful with my sister because she is little and can get hurt more easily.

USE OF LANGUAGE CONVENTIONS
The writer's use of pronouns is confusing. After referring to "my sister," she then addresses the sister directly as "you." Later, it is not clear who "He" is.

DEVELOPMENT OF IDEAS
In her conclusion, the writer explains what she learned from her experience. However, the narrative is not developed effectively.

Name ______________________________ Date ______________

Personal Narrative 2: Score Summary and Rubric **Score Point 2**

This personal narrative describes a series of events in chronological order and explains what the writer learned from her experience. However, it lacks focus and has few engaging details. Sentences are generally short, with several run-ons. Grammatical errors may confuse readers.

	ORGANIZATION/ PROGRESSION	DEVELOPMENT OF IDEAS	USE OF LANGUAGE CONVENTIONS
4	• Uses appropriate structure or form for purpose and demands of prompt; narrative strategies enhance effectiveness of writing • Uses details effectively; sustains focus, creating unity and coherence • Controls progression with transitions showing relationships among ideas	• Employs specific, well-chosen details that develop key literary elements • Engages reader through a thoughtful narrative that may approach topic from an unusual perspective; demonstrates a deep understanding of prompt	• Shows strong understanding of word choice appropriate to form, purpose, and tone • Uses purposeful, varied, and controlled sentences • Demonstrates command of conventions so that narrative is fluent and clear even if the writing contains minor errors
3	• Uses mostly effective structure or form for demands of prompt; narrative strategies generally enhance effectiveness of writing • Mostly uses details effectively; narrative is coherent though may lack overall unity • Mostly controls progression of ideas with transitions	• Employs specific details that add some substance to the narrative; details generally contribute to key literary elements • Demonstrates some depth of thought, with an original rather than formulaic approach and a good understanding of the task	• Shows basic understanding of word choice appropriate to form, purpose, and tone; diction generally succeeds in communicating meaning • Uses varied and mostly controlled sentences • Demonstrates general command of conventions; errors do not seriously affect clarity or fluency of narrative
2	• May use form or structure inappropriate to demands of the prompt; narrative strategies contribute only marginally to effectiveness • May use some details that do not contribute to narrative; focus may not be sustained • Controls progression of thought inconsistently; may lack clear links among ideas	• Fails to develop narrative beyond a minimal level because details may be inappropriate or incompletely developed; details only marginally contribute to key literary elements • Uses somewhat formulaic approach to prompt, reflecting limited understanding of task	• Shows limited understanding of word choice; may use basic or simplistic vocabulary • May use awkward, uncontrolled sentences • Demonstrates partial command of conventions, possibly with significant errors that weaken the fluency of writing
1	• Uses inappropriate form or structure • Lacks focus and apt details; coherence/unity are weak • Has weak progression of thought, with lack of meaningful transitions	• Exhibits weak development of ideas because details and examples are inappropriate, vague, or insufficient • Demonstrates lack of understanding of prompt and/ or vague approach	• Lacks appropriate word choice; uses imprecise or general vocabulary • Uses simplistic, awkward, or uncontrolled sentences • Demonstrates limited or no command of conventions

Name ______________________________ Date ______________

Written Composition: Expository Essay 1

READ

If you know how to do something well, you might want to teach a friend how to do it, too. Or, if you've worked hard to develop the perfect procedure for making something, you might like to share your expertise with others. Writing an expository essay is one way to do this.

THINK

Think of something you know how to do well. How would you explain to someone else how to do it? Consider all the details you would need to include so that the other person could do the task on his or her own.

WRITE

Write an expository essay that explains the procedure for a task that you can do well.

As you write your composition, remember to —

- ☐ focus on a controlling idea for a procedure that you can do well
- ☐ organize your response to that each step of the process is described clearly and in order, using transitions such as *first, next,* and *finally*
- ☐ develop your ideas fully and thoughtfully, including appropriate facts and details to make the process clear for the reader
- ☐ make sure your composition is no longer than one page

TEKS 14B, 14C, 14D, 17A, 19, 21

ANALYZE THE PROMPT
The prompt asks you to explain a procedure to communicate information. This means you should not write a story, a description, or your opinion about something.

RESPOND TO THE PROMPT

- **Plan** your draft by jotting down tasks you know how to do well. Choose the one you can explain most clearly. List key steps in the process.
- **Draft** your response by explaining steps in a logical order. Include helpful background information and descriptive details the reader needs to know.
- **Revise** to make the steps in the procedure clearer, to use more precise wording, to vary the lengths and types of sentences you use, and to add transitions connecting ideas.
- **Edit** your writing to make sure errors won't keep the reader from understanding what you have to say.

Name ______________________________ Date ______________

Benchmark Composition: Expository Essay 1

Score Point 4

A Smooth Procedure

Living in an old house with my do-it-yourself parents, I've learned a lot of strange skills. I may be one of the few 12-year-olds who knows how to do what's called taping and floating walls. Walls may seem solid and strong, but they're made of big sheets of thick paper surrounding a kind of plaster. This plaster can crack if the foundation of a house shifts a lot, or if a little brother (yes, mine) pretending to be a superhero bashes his head into the wall. Once the plaster cracks, it has to be repaired by taping and floating.

ORGANIZATION/ PROGRESSION
In the introduction, the writer clearly states the controlling idea.

DEVELOPMENT OF IDEAS
Specific details provide background about why the procedure is important. The writer also engages readers with an amusing real-life reason for repairing a crack.

The supplies needed to repair a crack are joint compound, a small container, seam tape, and a trowel. The first step is to put some joint compound into the container and use the trowel to mix in some water. Joint compound is also called "mud" for a good reason. Mixing it with water is like making mud pies, but the consistency has to be just right for it to smoothly cover a crack. If the mixed "mud" is too thick or too runny, adding more water or joint compound will make it smooth.

ORGANIZATION/ PROGRESSION
Meaningful transitions make the order of steps clear.

The next step is to use the trowel to spread joint compound along the crack. Sliding the trowel at an angle helps to make a smooth layer. Next, it's time to measure and tear the seam tape. The tape should be placed along the crack, making sure that the layer of joint compound covers the area under the tape completely.

Finally, more joint compound should be spread on top of the seam tape to cover it completely. The trowel should slide at an angle to smooth the joint compound away from the crack so that the repair will blend in with the surface of the wall. After drying for 24 hours, the repair can be sanded and painted. Then it will look like nothing ever happened—at least until the next little brother superhero adventure!

Name ______________________________ Date ______________

Expository Essay 1: Score Summary and Rubric **Score Point 4**

This essay successfully communicates information about a procedure. The writer provides an engaging introduction and background information to grab the reader's interest in the task. A clear step-by-step organization with transitions makes it clear how the task is done. Precise descriptions (*"mud," runny*) effectively communicate key information. The writer maintains a friendly, knowledgeable tone throughout the composition.

	ORGANIZATION/ PROGRESSION	DEVELOPMENT OF IDEAS	USE OF LANGUAGE CONVENTIONS
4	• Uses appropriate structure for purpose and demands of prompt • Establishes and sustains focus, unity, and coherence via controlling idea • Controls progression with transitions showing relationships among ideas	• Employs specific and well-chosen details and examples • Engages the reader through thoughtful development of ideas; may approach topic from an unusal perspective; demonstrates a deep understanding of prompt	• Shows understanding of word choice appropriate to purpose and intended tone • Uses purposeful, varied, and controlled sentences • Demonstrates a command of conventions so that essay is rhetorically effective even if it contains minor errors
3	• Uses mostly effective structure for purpose and demands of prompt • Relates most ideas to controlling idea; essay is coherent though may lack overall unity • Mostly controls progression of ideas with transitions	• Employs specific, appropriate details and examples that add some substance to essay • Demonstrates some depth of thought, with an original rather than formulaic approach and a good understanding of the task	• Shows basic understanding of word choice, appropriate to purpose and intended tone • Uses varied and generally controlled sentences • Demonstrates general command of conventions; errors do not seriously affect clarity or fluency
2	• May use structure that is inappropriate to prompt; structure may not contribute to clarity of explanation • May use weak or unclear controlling idea, reducing focus and coherence • Has inconsistent progression of thought, with too few meaningful transitions and connections	• Lacks strong development of ideas because details are inappropriate or insufficiently developed • Demonstrates little depth of thought, with a formulaic approach to the prompt and a limited understanding of the task	• Shows limited grasp of word choice, failing to establish appropriate tone • Uses awkward or uncontrolled sentences, weakening essay's effectiveness • Demonstrates partial command of conventions; errors may result in a lack of fluency or clarity
1	• Uses inappropriate or no obvious structure • Lacks clear controlling idea, with resulting weak focus and coherence • Has weak progression of thought, with lack of meaningful transitions and connections among ideas	• Lacks strong development of ideas because details and examples are inappropriate, vague, or insufficient • Demonstrates lack of understanding of prompt through an overall insubtantial essay and/or a vague or confused approach	• Lacks understanding of word choice; vocabulary is imprecise or unsuitable • Uses simplistic, awkward, or uncontrolled sentences, weakening essay's effectiveness • Demonstrates limited or no command of conventions, resulting in a lack of fluency

Name _______________________________ Date ______________

Benchmark Composition: Expository Essay 1

Score Point 2

Taking Care of the Best Cat in the World

One thing I know how to do really well is to take care of my cat. We got her as a kitten when I was 8. She's a tortoise-shell tabby, which means that her fur is a mix of many different colors. She doesn't look like any other cat. Unlike most cats, she's very friendly and enjoys hanging out with people and even dogs. She's also really good and loving so that makes her easy to take care of.

The main things you have to do to take care of a cat are to make sure they have plenty of food and water and to clean their litter box, which is nobody's favorite job. What makes me really good at it, though, is that I wear latex gloves and a breathing mask. It's still gross but at least I know I'm not touching or inhaling anything that could make me sick. My reward for that is that she likes to curl up in my lap, purring. I do the work so I get the benefit.

If anyone ever needs advice on how to take care of a cat, I can tell them all about it.

ORGANIZATION/ PROGRESSION
The purpose for writing is stated in the first sentence, but much of the information in the introduction is unnecessary and does little to support this purpose.

DEVELOPMENT OF IDEAS
The body of the essay states the tasks required for the procedure but does not develop or support them with details.

ORGANIZATION/ PROGRESSION
The conclusion attempts to wrap up the writer's ideas.

Name ______________________________ Date ______________

Expository Essay 1: Score Summary and Rubric **Score Point 2**

This essay communicates minimal information about a procedure. The introduction describes the cat rather than identifying the procedure. The body describes the supplies needed for two tasks, but there is no step-by-step information about how to perform the tasks. The few grammatical errors do not detract from the message. A brief conclusion provides no additional insights.

	ORGANIZATION/ PROGRESSION	DEVELOPMENT OF IDEAS	USE OF LANGUAGE CONVENTIONS
4	• Uses appropriate structure for purpose and demands of prompt • Establishes and sustains focus, unity, and coherence via controlling idea • Controls progression with transitions showing relationships among ideas	• Employs specific and well-chosen details and examples • Engages the reader through thoughtful development of ideas; may approach topic from an unusal perspective; demonstrates a deep understanding of prompt	• Shows understanding of word choice appropriate to purpose and intended tone • Uses purposeful, varied, and controlled sentences • Demonstrates a command of conventions so that essay is rhetorically effective even if it contains minor errors
3	• Uses mostly effective structure for purpose and demands of prompt • Relates most ideas to controlling idea; essay is coherent though may lack overall unity • Mostly controls progression of ideas with transitions	• Employs specific, appropriate details and examples that add some substance to essay • Demonstrates some depth of thought, with an original rather than formulaic approach and a good understanding of the task	• Shows basic understanding of word choice, appropriate to purpose and intended tone • Uses varied and generally controlled sentences • Demonstrates general command of conventions; errors do not seriously affect clarity or fluency
2	• May use structure that is inappropriate to prompt; structure may not contribute to clarity of explanation • May use weak or unclear controlling idea, reducing focus and coherence • Has inconsistent progression of thought, with too few meaningful transitions and connections	• Lacks strong development of ideas because details are inappropriate or insufficiently developed • Demonstrates little depth of thought, with a formulaic approach to the prompt and a limited understanding of the task	• Shows limited grasp of word choice, failing to establish appropriate tone • Uses awkward or uncontrolled sentences, weakening essay's effectiveness • Demonstrates partial command of conventions; errors may result in a lack of fluency or clarity
1	• Uses inappropriate or no obvious structure • Lacks clear controlling idea, with resulting weak focus and coherence • Has weak progression of thought, with lack of meaningful transitions and connections among ideas	• Lacks strong development of ideas because details and examples are inappropriate, vague, or insufficient • Demonstrates lack of understanding of prompt through an overall insubtantial essay and/or a vague or confused approach	• Lacks understanding of word choice; vocabulary is imprecise or unsuitable • Uses simplistic, awkward, or uncontrolled sentences, weakening essay's effectiveness • Demonstrates limited or no command of conventions, resulting in a lack of fluency

Name ______________________________ Date ______________

Written Composition: Expository Essay 2

READ

Some people like their tacos in a crispy shell. Others like a soft taco with a flour tortilla. And some people think it's even more fun to make tacos than to eat them.

THINK

Think about a food that you love to make or to eat. What is fun or interesting about the steps you take to prepare or eat this food? How would you explain your process to someone else?

WRITE

Write an expository essay that explains how to prepare or eat one of your favorite foods.

As you write your composition, remember to —

- ☐ focus on a controlling idea about how to prepare or eat one of your favorite foods
- ☐ organize your response so that each step of the process is described clearly and in order, using transitions such as *first, next,* and *finally*
- ☐ develop your ideas fully, including appropriate details and examples to make the process clear for the reader
- ☐ make sure your composition is no longer than one page

TEKS 14B, 14C, 14D, 17A, 19, 20, 21

ANALYZE THE PROMPT

The prompt asks you to explain a process. This means you should focus on the information readers will need to complete the process, without unnecessary description or personal opinions.

RESPOND TO THE PROMPT

- **Plan** by jotting down several foods you enjoying making or eating. Select one that involves a process of at least four steps. List the steps in the process.
- **Draft** your response by explaining the steps in the correct order. Include an introduction that tells readers why they would want to follow your instructions.
- **Revise** to make the steps in your process clearer, to use more precise wording, to vary your sentence types, and to add transitions connecting ideas.
- **Edit** your writing to correct any errors that would prevent readers from understanding what you have to say.

Name ______________________________ Date ______________

Benchmark Composition: Expository Essay 2

Score Point 4

Taming the Prickly Artichoke

The first time my mom stopped her grocery cart in front of the artichoke display, all I could say was "What are those?" I couldn't believe she planned to serve the prickly green things for dinner. Since that night, however, I've grown to love artichokes, including the process of preparing them. All the equipment you need is a pair of kitchen scissors, a cutting board, a sharp knife, and a large pot.

ORGANIZATION/ PROGRESSION
In the introduction, the writer clearly establishes the focus of his essay.

The first step is to rinse each artichoke under running water. Next, pull off the small leaves at the base of the artichoke, which are often discolored. Then, use the kitchen scissors to clip off the thorny tip of each leaf. (It's not really necessary to remove the thorns, because they become soft when you cook the artichokes. But I think the artichokes look nicer on your plate without the thorns.) Once the thorns are removed, use your knife to cut off most of the stem, leaving it about an inch long. Then turn the artichoke around and cut off the pointy tip.

DEVELOPMENT OF IDEAS
After an engaging introduction that lists the equipment readers will need, the writer presents the steps of the process in order. He uses transitions to help readers see the connections between steps.

When all of your artichokes have been washed and trimmed, they're ready to cook. Put two inches of water in your pot. I like to add a couple of peeled garlic cloves to the water. Then place your artichokes in the pot and bring the water to a boil. Reduce the heat, and then simmer the artichokes until the outer leaves can be pulled off easily. This can take anywhere from 25 to 45 minutes.

DEVELOPMENT OF IDEAS
The writer includes specific details that will help readers complete the process successfully.

My favorite way to eat artichokes is to simply dip each leaf in melted butter and then scrape off the tender flesh with my lower teeth. Yum! Now that you know the basic preparation technique, you can explore other delicious dips. The most important thing is to give artichokes a try—they're not as prickly as they look!

ORGANIZATION/ PROGRESSION
The conclusion emphasizes the reason readers might want to try this process—artichokes are delicious!

Name ______________________________ Date ______________

Expository Essay 2: Score Summary and Rubric **Score Point 4**

This expository essay successfully communicates how to complete a procedure. An engaging introduction captures readers' interest. The steps are presented in order using precise language and a fluent style. The writer provides all the necessary details to help readers perform the task on their own.

	ORGANIZATION/ PROGRESSION	DEVELOPMENT OF IDEAS	USE OF LANGUAGE CONVENTIONS
4	• Uses appropriate structure for purpose and demands of prompt • Establishes and sustains focus, unity, and coherence via controlling idea • Controls progression with transitions showing relationships among ideas	• Employs specific and well-chosen details and examples • Engages the reader through thoughtful development of ideas; may approach topic from an unusal perspective; demonstrates a deep understanding of prompt	• Shows understanding of word choice appropriate to purpose and intended tone • Uses purposeful, varied, and controlled sentences • Demonstrates a command of conventions so that essay is rhetorically effective even if it contains minor errors
3	• Uses mostly effective structure for purpose and demands of prompt • Relates most ideas to controlling idea; essay is coherent though may lack overall unity • Mostly controls progression of ideas with transitions	• Employs specific, appropriate details and examples that add some substance to essay • Demonstrates some depth of thought, with an original rather than formulaic approach and a good understanding of the task	• Shows basic understanding of word choice, appropriate to purpose and intended tone • Uses varied and generally controlled sentences • Demonstrates general command of conventions; errors do not seriously affect clarity or fluency
2	• May use structure that is inappropriate to prompt; structure may not contribute to clarity of explanation • May use weak or unclear controlling idea, reducing focus and coherence • Has inconsistent progression of thought, with too few meaningful transitions and connections	• Lacks strong development of ideas because details are inappropriate or insufficiently developed • Demonstrates little depth of thought, with a formulaic approach to the prompt and a limited understanding of the task	• Shows limited grasp of word choice, failing to establish appropriate tone • Uses awkward or uncontrolled sentences, weakening essay's effectiveness • Demonstrates partial command of conventions; errors may result in a lack of fluency or clarity
1	• Uses inappropriate or no obvious structure • Lacks clear controlling idea, with resulting weak focus and coherence • Has weak progression of thought, with lack of meaningful transitions and connections among ideas	• Lacks strong development of ideas because details and examples are inappropriate, vague, or insufficient • Demonstrates lack of understanding of prompt through an overall insubtantial essay and/or a vague or confused approach	• Lacks understanding of word choice; vocabulary is imprecise or unsuitable • Uses simplistic, awkward, or uncontrolled sentences, weakening essay's effectiveness • Demonstrates limited or no command of conventions, resulting in a lack of fluency

Name ______________________________ Date ______________

Benchmark Composition: Expository Essay 2

Score Point 2

How to Make Banana Bread

Making banana bread is easy and its delicious. My uncle taught me how to do it. He lives in Cleveland but when he visits we make banana bread together. You can make banana bread to.

Mix 3 or four bananas with 1/3 cup butter first melt the butter and mash the bananas then add a cup of sugar an egg and a teaspoon of vanilla. After mixing in a teaspoon of baking soda and a little salt add the flour. we use all-purpose but whole-wheat can be good if you like a denser kind of bread. Preheat the oven and put the batter in a loaf pan that's been buttered. My little brother and sister like to butter the pan because they think it's like finger painting, but my mom told me I shouldnt let them make a mess in the kitchen. Bake for an hour or until its done. Cool on a rack and keep the little kids away until it cools. Some people like to add walnuts to their banana bread. Enjoy!

USE OF LANGUAGE CONVENTIONS
Grammatical errors like this run-on sentence make the essay difficult to understand.

DEVELOPMENT OF IDEAS
The writer describes steps in a process, but they are not presented in a clear order. Some details are included that distract from the purpose of the essay.

Name ______________________________ Date ______________

Expository Essay 2: Score Summary and Rubric **Score Point 2**

This expository essay describes a process, but a reader would have difficulty following the instructions. Steps are presented out of order *(Mix 3 or four bananas with 1/3 cup butter first melt the butter and mash the bananas),* and some key details (such as the exact amount of flour) are omitted.

	ORGANIZATION/ PROGRESSION	DEVELOPMENT OF IDEAS	USE OF LANGUAGE CONVENTIONS
4	• Uses appropriate structure for purpose and demands of prompt • Establishes and sustains focus, unity, and coherence via controlling idea • Controls progression with transitions showing relationships among ideas	• Employs specific and well-chosen details and examples • Engages the reader through thoughtful development of ideas; may approach topic from an unusal perspective; demonstrates a deep understanding of prompt	• Shows understanding of word choice appropriate to purpose and intended tone • Uses purposeful, varied, and controlled sentences • Demonstrates a command of conventions so that essay is rhetorically effective even if it contains minor errors
3	• Uses mostly effective structure for purpose and demands of prompt • Relates most ideas to controlling idea; essay is coherent though may lack overall unity • Mostly controls progression of ideas with transitions	• Employs specific, appropriate details and examples that add some substance to essay • Demonstrates some depth of thought, with an original rather than formulaic approach and a good understanding of the task	• Shows basic understanding of word choice, appropriate to purpose and intended tone • Uses varied and generally controlled sentences • Demonstrates general command of conventions; errors do not seriously affect clarity or fluency
2	• May use structure that is inappropriate to prompt; structure may not contribute to clarity of explanation • May use weak or unclear controlling idea, reducing focus and coherence • Has inconsistent progression of thought, with too few meaningful transitions and connections	• Lacks strong development of ideas because details are inappropriate or insufficiently developed • Demonstrates little depth of thought, with a formulaic approach to the prompt and a limited understanding of the task	• Shows limited grasp of word choice, failing to establish appropriate tone • Uses awkward or uncontrolled sentences, weakening essay's effectiveness • Demonstrates partial command of conventions; errors may result in a lack of fluency or clarity
1	• Uses inappropriate or no obvious structure • Lacks clear controlling idea, with resulting weak focus and coherence • Has weak progression of thought, with lack of meaningful transitions and connections among ideas	• Lacks strong development of ideas because details and examples are inappropriate, vague, or insufficient • Demonstrates lack of understanding of prompt through an overall insubtantial essay and/or a vague or confused approach	• Lacks understanding of word choice; vocabulary is imprecise or unsuitable • Uses simplistic, awkward, or uncontrolled sentences, weakening essay's effectiveness • Demonstrates limited or no command of conventions, resulting in a lack of fluency

Name ______________________________ Date ______________

Written Composition Practice: Personal Narrative 1

READ

Making a big change is often difficult or even painful. However, change helps us learn new things and grow as people. For this reason, times of change are often the most important times in our lives.

THINK

Think about a time when your life changed significantly or you made a fresh start. How did you feel about this change at the time? How did the change affect your life?

WRITE

Write a personal narrative about a change or a new beginning in your life that was important to you.

As you write your composition, remember to —

- ☐ focus on a controlling idea that reflects an important change or new beginning in your life
- ☐ organize your ideas logically and link them with transitions
- ☐ develop your ideas fully and thoughtfully, including the significance of the event
- ☐ make sure your composition is no longer than one page

Name ______________________ Date ______________

Written Composition Practice: Personal Narrative 2

READ

It's great to know how to do something and be able to do it independently. However, sometimes we need help from someone else to accomplish a goal.

THINK

Think of a time when another person helped you do something that was important to you. Why did you need help to reach your goal? How did the other person help you?

WRITE

Write a personal narrative about a person who helped you accomplish something.

As you write your composition, remember to —

- ☐ focus on a controlling idea about the importance of this person's help in accomplishing your goal
- ☐ organize your ideas logically and link them with transitions
- ☐ develop your ideas fully and thoughtfully, including why you needed help and how the person helped you
- ☐ make sure your composition is no longer than one page

Name ______________________________ Date ____________________

Written Composition Practice: Expository Essay 1

READ

For students, summer vacation provides a relaxing break between one grade and the next. There are fun things to do and plenty of free time. On the other hand, sleeping until noon every day has its drawbacks.

THINK

Think about how you spend your summer vacations. Consider the fun times as well as the boring times. How do you feel in the fall when you suddenly have to get back on your school schedule?

WRITE

Write an expository essay that discusses the good and bad points about having a summer vacation from school.

As you write your composition, remember to —

- ☐ focus on a controlling idea that reflects both good and bad points about having a summer vacation from school
- ☐ organize ideas logically and link them with transitions
- ☐ develop your ideas fully and thoughtfully, including appropriate facts and details to illustrate your points
- ☐ make sure your composition is no longer than one page

Name ______________________________ Date ______________

Written Composition Practice: Expository Essay 2

READ

Clothing serves many purposes. Some clothing is stylish, some keeps us warm, and some shows our respect on formal occasions.

THINK

Think of an event or activity that requires very specific clothing. How do you select the right things to wear? What is the purpose of each item, and how do the items work together?

WRITE

Write an expository essay that explains how to select the proper clothing for a particular event or activity.

As you write your composition, remember to —

- ☐ establish a controlling idea about the importance of selecting the proper clothing for the particular event or activity
- ☐ organize your response so that each step of the process is presented clearly and in order, using transitions such as *first, next,* and *last*
- ☐ develop your ideas fully, including appropriate details and examples to make the process clear for the reader
- ☐ make sure your composition is no longer than one page

Revising and Editing

Name ______________________________ Date ______________

Guided Revising

Read the following personal narrative. Then read each question and mark the correct answer.

Tim wrote this personal narrative about what happened when his grandfather died and why it was important. He would like you to read his narrative and think about the improvements he should make. When you finish reading, answer the questions that follow.

Losing Grandpa

(1) "Wake up, Tim."

(2) "What time is it?" I asked.

(3) "About eleven-thirty," she answered.

(4) "Eleven-thirty? At night?" (5) I just knew something horrible had happened.

(6) "Why did you wake me up?"

(7) "Grandma just called."

(8) "Which one?"

(9) "Grandma Coberly."

(10) Suddenly I felt a chill. (11) My Grandma and Grandpa Coberly were older and more frail than my other grandparents.

(12) "What did she say?" I asked.

(13) "Grandpa's in the hospital. (14) He had a heart attack."

(15) "Is he okay?"

(16) "It doesn't look good," Mom replied.

(17) At that moment, I wondered why everyone always says "It doesn't look good" instead of saying what they really mean.

(18) On the way to the funeral in Phoenix, I kept hoping that Grandpa wasn't really gone and that I would see him as soon as I got off the plane.

(19) The weather was nice on the day of the funeral. (20) On television, funerals always happen on rainy days. (21) I was angry that my grandpa was buried on such a nice day.

(22) I cried all the way back to my grandma's house. (23) My grandma's house was very small. (24) I kept thinking about the times Grandpa took me fishing. (25) It was the first time someone close to me had died.

GO ON

Name ______________________________ Date ________________

1 Tim wants to make the conversation that begins his narrative easier to understand. What change, if any, should he make?

A Move sentence 1 to just before sentence 8

B Delete sentences 1–4

C Following sentence 1, add the sentence **My mom gently shook me awake.**

D Make no change

> **EXPLANATION:** Readers need more information to understand who is talking. The correct answer is **C.**
> - **A** is incorrect. Moving sentence 1 won't help identify who is speaking.
> - **B** is incorrect. Deleting sentences 1–4 won't help the narrative, especially since the dialogue continues in sentence 6.
> - **D** is incorrect. It is unclear who is speaking, so revision is necessary.

TEKS 14C

2 Tim would like to add information to help readers understand the events in his narrative. Which sentence should Tim add before sentence 18 to make his narrative clearer?

F I couldn't go back to sleep.

G I wanted to ask Mom what she meant.

H I hoped Grandpa would be all right.

J My grandfather died that night.

> **EXPLANATION:** The reader needs to know before reading sentence 18 that Tim's grandfather died. The correct answer is **J.**
> - **F, G,** and **H** are all incorrect because they don't tell the reader that Grandpa Coberly has died.

TEKS 14C

3 To help readers picture the setting, what is the best way for Tim to revise sentence 19?

A The weather was warm and sunny on the day of the funeral.

B The weather was cloudy on the day of the funeral.

C The weather was horrible on the day of the funeral.

D The weather was like any other day on the day of the funeral.

> **EXPLANATION:** From reading sentences 20 and 21, readers will know that the weather was not rainy. However, they will not know exactly what Tim means by "nice." The correct answer is **A.**
> - **B** and **C** are incorrect because they both describe conditions that are the opposite of nice.
> - **D** is incorrect because it is unclear what kind of weather "any other day" describes—sunny or rainy.

TEKS 14C

4 Which sentence does not belong in this personal narrative?

F Sentence 5

G Sentence 21

H Sentence 23

J Sentence 24

> **EXPLANATION:** The description of Grandma's house has nothing to do with Grandpa Coberly's death or how it affected Tim. The correct answer is **H.**
> - **F, G,** and **J** are all incorrect because they describe how Tim reacted when his grandfather became ill and died.

TEKS 14C

STOP

Name ______________________________ Date ______________

Revising Practice 1

Read the following personal narrative. Then read each question and mark the correct answer.

Selena wrote this personal narrative about hiking with her stepsister in Colorado. She would like you to read her narrative and think about the improvements she should make. When you finish reading, answer the questions that follow.

The Long Hike

(1) I could feel the perspiration flowing down my reddened face as I trudged along the trail. (2) I looked at my new stepsister. (3) She was effortlessly hiking up the steep, winding path. (4) It wasn't fair.

(5) I thought back to the day when my mother announced our vacation plans for the summer. (6) We were going to spend a week hiking in Colorado and exploring the Continental Divide. (7) I had read about the Continental Divide in my social studies class. (8) I made an effort to look excited as Mom described the challenging trails. (9) Kate didn't have to try. (10) She was genuinely happy about sleeping with bugs and hiking up a dirty trail. (11) She loved being outdoors. (12) I preferred being inside with the air conditioning blowing.

(13) A loud yell interrupted my thoughts and brought me back to the present. (14) Kate had made it to the top of the incline. (15) She looked down at me with a grin on her face. (16) When I frowned, her smile faded. (17) Everything seemed so easy for Kate. (18) I was filled with jealousy and I wanted to go home.

(19) I continued to climb even though my legs felt like rubber. (20) She began to tell me about her first day at our school. (21) She explained that every teacher compared her to me. (22) She also told me that all the girls told her stories about how funny I am. (23) She felt that she could never be as smart and witty as I am.

(24) I thought about what she said. (25) It seemed that Kate felt the same way I did. (26) Suddenly the trail did not seem as difficult. (27) I looked over at Kate and gave her a big smile. (28) On that day I realized that we were both special in our own way.

GO ON

Name ______________________________ Date ______________

1 Selena wants to add variety to her narrative by combining sentences. How should she combine sentences 11 and 12 to highlight the differences between Kate and her?

- **A** She loved being outdoors; indeed, I preferred being inside with the air conditioning blowing.
- **B** She loved being outdoors; therefore, I preferred being inside with the air conditioning blowing.
- **C** She loved being outdoors, while I preferred being inside with the air conditioning blowing.
- **D** She loved being outdoors because I preferred being inside with the air conditioning blowing.

2 Selena wants to replace *loud* in sentence 13 with a more precise word. Which word should she use to describe Kate's yell?

- **F** joyful
- **G** painful
- **H** muffled
- **J** fearful

3 Which sentence should Selena add before sentence 20 to make the sequence of events in her narrative clearer?

- **A** I wish I had the strength to go on.
- **B** When I reached the top, I sat down across from Kate.
- **C** I turned around and headed down the trail.
- **D** Kate started down the trail before I reached the top.

4 Which sentence should Selena delete because it does not relate to her main point?

- **F** She was effortlessly hiking up the steep winding path.
- **G** We were going to spend a week hiking in Colorado and exploring the Continental Divide.
- **H** I had read about the Continental Divide in my social studies class.
- **J** I continued to climb even though my legs felt like rubber.

STOP

Name ______________________________ Date ______________

Revising Practice 2

Read the following personal narrative. Then read each question and mark the correct answer.

Ryan wrote this personal narrative about his experience serving the community. He would like you to read his narrative and look for improvements he should make. When you finish reading, answer the questions that follow.

The Garden

(1) I cannot believe my bad luck. (2) I will be working at the Beachtown Community Garden. (3) I will be working there for the next two weeks. (4) Mrs. Lance, who is our teacher, gave us a new assignment today. (5) Our assignment is to help the community. (6) She wrote down different ways we could help and put them in a hat. (7) I drew the garden. (8) Yuck!

(9) I drag my feet as I walk to the park. (10) The garden is in a section of the park next to the Duck Pond. (11) I open the gate and walk inside. (12) The garden has hundreds of tiny green plants. (13) I let out a sigh just thinking about the dirt that will cover my favorite shoes.

(14) Mrs. Carson, the garden director, comes over and introduces herself. (15) She tells me that each day I have to pick weeds and water the plants.

(16) As I start to water, I look over at an elderly man. (17) He is bent over carefully picking weeds. (18) I wonder why he is here. (19) He looks up and smiles. (20) I give a little wave and return to my watering.

(21) After an hour, the man walks over and introduces himself as Albert. (22) He comes to the garden every day and waters, picks weeds, and harvests vegetables. (23) My favorite vegetables are tomatoes. (24) I ask him why he comes to the Beachtown garden each day. (25) He looks surprised at my question.

(26) "I volunteer here because the food is grown for people who cannot afford to buy food of their own," he explained.

(27) Suddenly, the dirt on my shoes does not seem very important. (28) As I pick up my hose, this time I carefully water each tiny little plant.

GO ON

Name ______________________________ Date ______________

1 Ryan wants to replace *bad* in sentence 1 with a more descriptive word. Which word should he use to describe his luck?

A rotten
B horrific
C unusual
D shocking

2 Ryan wants to add variety to his sentence beginnings. What is the most effective way for him to combine sentences 2 and 3?

F My work will be at the Beachtown Community Garden for the next two weeks.
G For the next two weeks, I will be working at the Beachtown Community Garden.
H The Beachtown Community Garden is where I'll be working for the next two weeks.
J I will be working for the next two weeks; it will be at the Beachtown Community Garden.

3 Ryan wants his audience to understand why he was unhappy about his assignment. Which sentence should Ryan add after sentence 8 make this clear?

A Work is boring.
B I hate getting dirty.
C Community service is a waste of time.
D My teacher always gives me the worst jobs.

4 Which transitional phrase should Ryan add to the beginning of sentence 11 to make the sequence of events in his narrative clearer?

F After I pass the path,
G Once I see the pond,
H When I get to the garden,
J Before I walk through the park,

5 Which sentence should be deleted from this personal narrative?

A Sentence 20
B Sentence 21
C Sentence 22
D Sentence 23

6 Ryan wants to add information to help readers understand the reason for his changed attitude. Which sentence should he add after sentence 27 to make his narrative clearer?

F My mom could wash off the dirt for me.
G Many people go to food banks to get food.
H I think about the people in my community who are hungry.
J Many other neighboring towns have community gardens.

STOP

Name ______________________________ Date ______________

Guided Editing

Read the following essay. Then read each question and mark the correct answer.

Asha wrote this expository essay about snakes. She would like you to read her essay and think about the corrections she should make. When you finish reading, answer the questions that follow.

The Truth About Snakes

(1) Do you think snakes are evil, slimy, scary creatures. (2) Many people do. (3) Throughout history, people have feared snakes because of its strange appearance and reputation for being poisonous. (4) However, many fears really are the result of false stories and false ideas.

(5) Snakes are members of the reptile family. (6) Like other reptiles, they are cold-blooded and their bodies are covered with scales. (7) Unlike most other reptiles, they don't have legs, movable eyelids, or outside ear openings. (8) Their appearance is probably their most interesting feature. (9) Their bodies are long, slender, and smooth.

(10) People often think snakes are slimy, like eels, but snakeskin is smooth and dry. (11) Many people also beleive all snakes are poisonous. (12) However, most snakes are harmless to humans. (13) One myth is that snakes slither across the ground at high speeds. (14) In fact, most snakes only go about one mile per hour. (15) Another myth tells about a hoop snake, which is supposed to form a hoop by taking its tail in its mouth. (16) Then it rolls down a hill and flings itself at its enemy. (17) Scientists say no such snakes exist.

(18) Despite these frightening images, snakes are actually useful animals. (19) Farmers use them to control pests such as mice and rats. (20) Even the venom of poisonous snakes aren't all bad. (21) It is used in medicines and for medical research. (22) Instead of fearing snakes, we should learn to appreciate them.

GO ON

Name ______________________________ Date ______________

1 What change, if any, should be made in sentence 1?

A Change the commas to semicolons

B Change ***scary*** to **scarey**

C Change the period to a question mark

D Make no change

EXPLANATION: Sentence 1 is a question and requires a question mark. The correct answer is **C.**

- **A** is incorrect. Commas are used to separate items in a series. Changing the commas to semicolons will create an error.
- **B** is incorrect. Changing the spelling of *scary* will create an error.
- **D** is incorrect. A change is necessary.

TEKS 14D, 20B, 21

2 Which change should be made in sentence 3?

F Delete the comma

G Change ***have*** to **has**

H Change ***its*** to **their**

J Change ***appearance*** to **apearance**

EXPLANATION: Pronouns should agree in number with the nouns to which they refer. The pronoun *its* is singular, but *snakes,* the noun to which it refers, is plural. The correct answer is **H.**

- **F** is incorrect. The comma is needed to set off the introductory phrase.
- **G** is incorrect. Changing *have* to *has* will create an error in subject-verb agreement.
- **J** is incorrect. Changing the spelling of *appearance* will create an error.

TEKS 14D, 20B, 21

3 What change, if any, should be made in sentence 11?

A Change ***beleive*** to **believe**

B Insert a comma after ***beleive***

C Change ***poisonous*** to **poisenous**

D Make no change

EXPLANATION: The word *beleive* is misspelled. The correct answer is **A.**

- **B** is incorrect because the sentence does not need a comma.
- **C** is incorrect because *poisonous* is spelled correctly.
- **D** is incorrect because a change is necessary.

TEKS 14D, 21

4 Which change should be made in sentence 20?

F Insert a comma after ***Even***

G Change ***venom*** to **venum**

H Change ***aren't*** to **isn't**

J Change the period to a question mark

EXPLANATION: Even when a subject and a verb are separated, the two should agree in number. The verb in this sentence should agree with *venom,* which is singular. The correct answer is **H.**

- **F** is incorrect because adding a comma after *Even* will create an error.
- **G** is incorrect because *venom* is the correct spelling.
- **J** is incorrect because a period is the correct punctuation for a statement.

TEKS 14D, 21

STOP

Name ______________________________ Date ______________

Editing Practice 1

Read the following essay. Then read each question and mark the correct answer.

Kang wrote this biographical essay about a famous mountain climber. He would like you to read his essay and think about the corrections he should make.

Keep Climbing

(1) On May 25, 2001, Erik Weihenmayer made history. (2) He climbed Mt. Everest the world's highest peak. (3) Climbing the mountain did not make Erik famous. (4) What was historic about the event was that Erik was the first blind person to accomplish the feat.

(5) Erik Weihenmayer lost his sight when he was thirteen years old. (6) Although he could no longer see. (7) Erik continued to pursue his goals and participate in the activities he enjoyed before he lost his sight. (8) One goal was to join his high school wrestling team. (9) He not only joined the team, but he is the captain. (10) Throughout his life, Erik would not let the loss of sight stop him from pursuing his athletic passions. (11) He enjoys paragliding, skiing, rock climbing, and running marathons.

(12) Erik also pursued his passion for education and teaching. (13) After graduating from high school he attended Boston College and became a middle school teacher. (14) He combined his love of teaching and mountain climbing and traveled to the country of tibet. (15) There he worked with a group called Braille Without Borders and taught blind teenagers to climb mountains.

(16) Climbing Mt. Everest is an amazing accomplishment. (17) What makes Erik's feat even more admirable is that he did not stop after reaching his goal. (18) After conquering Mt. Everest, he will set a goal to climb the Seven Summits, which are the highest peaks on every continent. (19) Erik Weihenmayer has accomplished that goal, and he continues to challenge himself every day with new and exciting adventures. (20) Erik is truly a remarkable person and athlete.

GO ON

Name ______________________________ Date ______________

1 Which change should be made in sentence 2?

A Change ***Mt. Everest*** to **Mt. everest**
B Insert a comma after ***Everest***
C Change ***climbed*** to **climbs**
D Delete the apostrophe in ***world's***

2 What change, if any, should be made in sentence 6?

F Change the period to a comma and add sentence 7 to the end of sentence 6
G Insert a comma after ***Although***
H Change the period at the end of the sentence to a question mark
J Make no change

3 What change, if any, should be made in sentence 9?

A Change ***is*** to **became**
B Delete the comma
C Change ***captain*** to **Captain**
D Make no change

4 What change, if any, should be made in sentence 14?

F Insert a comma after ***teaching***
G Change ***tibet*** to **Tibet**
H Insert a comma after ***climbing***
J Make no change

5 Which change should be made in sentence 18?

A Delete the comma after ***Everest***
B Delete the comma after ***Summits***
C Change ***Seven*** to **seven**
D Change ***will set*** to **set**

STOP

Name ______________________________ Date ______________

Editing Practice 2

Read the following letter. Then read each question and mark the correct answer.

Mark wrote this letter to share his ideas about a skate park with his teacher. He would like you to read his letter and think about the corrections he should make. When you finish reading, answer the questions that follow.

(1) Dear Mr. Richmond,

(2) Yesterday my friends and I went to town creek park. (3) We planned to ride our skateboards there. (4) However at the entrance to the park, I noticed a new sign: No Skateboards Allowed. (5) My friends and I were upset. (6) We went home to think of another place we could skate. (7) Unfortunately, we could not think of one place in our community that allows skateboards. (8) This is a problem for many young people in Forestville, but I think we have a solution.

(9) There is an abandoned lot on Sharp Street. (10) The lot is covered with weeds and trash. (11) Imagine if the weeds and trash were removed and replaced with clean ramps, sidewalks, and railings. (12) Sharp Street would be free of pollution and provide a safe place for skateboarders to skate.

(13) My friends and I have also thought about how the city might pay for the skate park. (14) The city could asking businesses to donate the materials to build the ramps. (15) Skateboarders could do chores such as raking leaves, and donate their money to the skate park. (16) If everyone works together, we can quickly raise enough money to build the park.

(17) Skateboarders in Forestville need a skate park. (18) It is not safe to ride on sidewalks in town because people also walking on the sidewalks. (19) Furthermore, skateboards are not allowed in parks, and the school board voted last week not to allow skateboards on school sidewalks. (20) Skaters need a safe place to skate.

(21) We think our idea for a skate park will help everyone in the community. (22) We could be happy to meet with you in person to explain our ideas. (23) Thank you for your time.

(24) Sincerely,

Mark

GO ON

Name ________________________________ Date ________________

1 What change, if any, should be made in sentence 2?

A Change ***I*** to **me**
B Change ***went*** to **go**
C Change ***town creek park*** to **Town Creek Park**
D Make no change

2 What change should be made in sentence 4?

F Insert a comma after ***However***
G Change ***park*** to **Park**
H Change ***noticed*** to **notice**
J Change ***new*** to **knew**

3 What change should be made in sentence 14?

A Change ***businesses*** to **busineses**
B Insert a semicolon after ***donate***
C Change ***build*** to **builds**
D Change ***asking*** to **ask**

4 What change, if any, should be made in sentence 15?

F Insert a comma after ***chores***
G Change ***raking*** to **rakes**
H Change ***their*** to **his**
J Make no change

5 What change should be made in sentence 18?

A Change ***because*** to **although**
B Change ***walking*** to **walk**
C Change ***ride*** to **rides**
D Insert a comma after ***safe***

6 What change, if any, should be made in sentence 22?

F Change ***could be*** to **would be**
G Change ***meet*** to **have met**
H Change ***explain*** to **explane**
J Make no change

STOP

Part II

Texas Write Source Assessments

Name ______________________________ Date ______________

Pretest

Part 1: Basic Elements of Writing

Questions 1–12: Read each sentence. Choose the best way to write the underlined part of the sentence. Fill in the circle of the correct answer on your answer document.

1 *Tyrannosaurus rex* was the larger meat-eating dinosaur on Earth.

A largerest
B large
C largest
D Make no change

2 *T. rex* stood nearly twenty feet in height.

F nearer twenty feet
G near twenty feet
H nearest twenty feet
J Make no change

3 Scientists has predicted *T. rex* weighed up to seven tons, or about 1,400 pounds!

A had predicts
B have predicted
C has predict
D Make no change

4 Although much larger and stronger, *T. rex's* legs was similar to those of today's birds.

F are
G were
H being
J Make no change

5 *T. rex* had scaly legs, long shins, so three toes that pointed forward.

A or
B but
C and
D Make no change

6 *T. rex* had a fourth toe, which pointed backwards on the heel.

F who
G whom
H that
J Make no change

7 Tyrannosaurus' hind legs were large and strong but there forelegs, or arms, were small and weak.

A their
B theirs
C they're
D Make no change

8 When you see a *T. rex* in the movies, it always roars fierce.

F fiercely
G fiercer
H fiercest
J Make no change

GO ON

Name ______________________________ Date ______________

9 Some of the scientists <u>which</u> study dinosaurs have determined that *T. rex* could not run very fast.

A whom
B whose
C who
D Make no change

10 *T. rex* had <u>amazing powerfully</u> jaws and keen eyesight.

F amazing powerfulest
G amazingly powerful
H amazingly powerfuler
J Make no change

11 A team of archaeologists <u>have being uncovering</u> a complete *T. rex* skeleton in South Dakota.

A have been uncovered
B had being uncovering
C has been uncovering
D Make no change

12 No one <u>have</u> ever seen such a well-preserved skeleton.

F has
G having
H haves
J Make no change

Questions 13–18: Read each question and fill in the circle of the correct answer on your answer document.

13 Which sentence contains an adjectival clause?

A Connor and his family enjoyed the baseball game because it was such a beautiful day.
B Even though the home team lost, they still had fun.
C They appreciated the seats that Connor picked, near the third base line.
D The home team fans booed the umpire the whole game.

14 Which is a run-on sentence that should be written as two sentences?

F Connor ate popcorn, peanuts, and a hot dog.
G He was very thirsty by the seventh inning when everyone got up to stretch.
H The lines at the snack bar were long, he just couldn't wait.
J Connor decided to get a drink at the water fountain and wait until later for a soda.

15 Which is the adverbial phrase in the sentence?

James prefers to finish his homework before his favorite television show airs.

A to finish his homework
B before his favorite television show airs
C James prefers to finish
D his favorite television show

GO ON

Name ______________________________ Date ______________

16 Which is the best way to combine these two sentences?

> Connor's mom and dad took turns scoring the game.
>
> They took turns watching Brooke.

F Connor's mom and dad took turns scoring the game; took turns watching Brooke.

G Connor's mom and Connor's dad took turns scoring and watching the game.

H Connor's mom and dad took turns scoring the game and watching Brooke.

J Connor's mom and dad took turns scoring the game, and they also took turns watching Brooke.

17 Which is an interrogative sentence that should end with a question mark?

A I wish my dad would take me to a game

B Do you like going to baseball games

C Connor's family can't wait until the next game

D They have already bought their tickets

18 Which is a complete sentence with parallel structure?

F John loves to play checkers, a baseball game, and to play video games.

G Mom says that television rots your brain, eyes, and to not watch it.

H The film was entertaining, informative, and well-received.

J Neither Will or Rohit like apple pie.

Questions 19–20: A student wrote this paragraph about summer camp. It may need some changes or corrections. Read the paragraph. Then read each question. Fill in the circle of the correct answer on your answer document.

Summer Camp Blues

This summer I went away to overnight camp for the first time. It was a new experience for me. The first few days at camp were the hardest. I missed my parents, my pet gerbils, and even my little brother. All I could think about was my family. Then I made a new friend, Jessie. She and I spent the next two weeks together. I didn't forget my family, but I stopped missing them and started having fun.

19 What type of paragraph is this?

A expository

B persuasive

C response to a text

D narrative

20 Which detail sentence would be best to add just before the last sentence in this paragraph?

F We hiked, went on canoe trips, and sang camp songs together.

G I even wrote home, asking my parents to come and get me.

H My counselors were nice.

J The director took the kids in our cabin to explore some caves.

GO ON

Name ______________________________ Date ______________

Part 2: Proofreading and Editing

Questions 21–30: Read the passages. Choose the best way to write each underlined part. Fill in the circle of the correct answer on your answer document.

Dear Ms. Russo: (21)

My name is Jason Weston. I am one of the students in Mr. Eriksons' (22) class at Memorial Middle School. I really enjoyed our field trip to the art museum; still, (23) I plan to return soon. What a fascinating place!

Now I am writing a report on painter Frida Kahlo and her works. My favorite painting of hers is Self-portrait with Monkeys. (24) Can you tell me how many Kahlo paintings the museum has? Thank you for your help.

Sincerely. (25)
Jason

21 **A** Ms. Russo,
B Ms. Russo;
C Ms. Russo!
D Make no change

22 **F** Mr. Erikson's
G Mr. Eriksons
H Mr. Eriksons's
J Make no change

23 **A** museum; for that reason,
B museum; otherwise,
C museum; besides,
D Make no change

24 **F** 'Self-portrait with Monkeys.'
G *Self-portrait with Monkeys*.
H "Self-portrait with Monkeys."
J Make no change

25 **A** Sincerely:
B Sincerely;
C Sincerely,
D Make no change

GO ON

Name ______________________ Date ______________

The sun is important to all living creatures. Plants and animals rely on the sun to survive. Plants use the sun to make <u>food. The process called photosynthesis.</u> (26) Animals rely on the food and <u>oxigen</u> (27) that plants make during photosynthesis. Cold-blooded animals also need the sun's warmth to heat up their bodies. That's why you often see turtles and snakes sunning <u>themselves</u> (28) on logs or rocks. Warm-blooded animals, such as <u>Humans and other Mammals</u>, (29) also need the sun for the vitamin D it provides. Without the sun, life as we know it <u>wouldn't never</u> (30) survive.

26 **F** food, The process called photosynthesis.
G food through a process called photosynthesis.
H food: the process called photosynthesis.
J Make no change

27 **A** oxygen
B oxijen
C oxyjen
D Make no change

28 **F** himself
G itself
H theirselves
J Make no change

29 **A** Humans and other mammals
B humans and other Mammals
C humans and other mammals
D Make no change

30 **F** would not never
G would never
H wouldn't not never
J Make no change

GO ON

Name ______________________________ Date ____________________

Part 3: Writing — Narrative

READ

People need few excuses to hold a celebration. Birthdays, weddings, graduations, anniversaries—we frequently celebrate these occasions and others. Celebrations can also take many forms, from modest and simple to large and spectacular.

THINK

Think back to a special celebration you took part in. What were you celebrating? Where, and with whom?

WRITE

Write a narrative essay describing what you did at that special celebration.

As you write your composition, remember to —

- ☐ focus on a controlling idea that reflects a special celebration you took part in
- ☐ organize your ideas logically and link them with transitions
- ☐ include appropriate facts and details about the event and communicate its importance
- ☐ make sure your composition is no longer than one page

STOP

Name ____________________ Date ____________

Progress Test 1

Part 1: Basic Elements of Writing

Questions 1–12: Read each sentence. Choose the best way to write the underlined part of the sentence. Fill in the circle of the correct answer on your answer document.

1 Marguerite is learning karate <u>from</u> Sensei Carlos.

A by
B at
C in
D Make no change

2 Everyone from young children to seniors <u>practice</u> it.

F practicing
G practices
H are practicing
J Make no change

3 Many martial arts, including karate, came from Asia <u>originally.</u>

A original
B originaler
C origin
D Make no change

4 <u>Student</u> of karate advance from white belts to black belts.

F Studentes
G Studying
H Students
J Make no change

5 Forms of karate <u>have been teached</u> in China for centuries.

A have been taught
B are being taught
C were teached
D Make no change

6 There are seven main colors for karate <u>belts;</u> white, yellow, orange, green, blue, brown, and black.

F belts,
G belts:
H belts.
J Make no change

7 My neighbor Lita, <u>that</u> is only eight years old, can break a wooden board with a kick.

A which
B whom
C who
D Make no change

8 Next month, Lita <u>was competing</u> in a karate tournament.

F competed
G will compete
H are competing
J Make no change

GO ON

Name ______________________ Date ______________

9 Lita's karate teacher is very pleased with their progress.

A her
B hers
C our
D Make no change

10 The walls in the dojo glimmers with trophies.

F glimmering
G glimmerses
H glimmer
J Make no change

11 Take karate might be fun for me, too.

A Takes
B Took
C Taking
D Make no change

12 Other martial arts seems easier to learn than karate.

F seem
G seeming
H is seeming
J Make no change

Questions 13–18: Read each question and fill in the circle of the correct answer on your answer document.

13 Which is a complete sentence written correctly?

A The sensei awarded the black belt to whom?
B Caleb's father whom studies at the Chicago dojo.
C Will was the only boy whom coughed all night.
D Snickering came from the crowd, whom formed along the bleachers.

14 Which of the following incudes the best transition for sentence to sentence coherence?

F Jeffrey and Sam are reading about wizards. They love fantasy novels.
G James and Peter can't stand fantasies. I think they will choose mysteries.
H Do you know James and Peter? What do you think you will choose?
J I might read a biography. However, my preference is to read historical fiction.

15 Which is the best way to combine these two sentences?

> Samantha likes comic books.
>
> Keisha does not like comic books.

A Samantha likes comic books, but Keisha does not.
B Samantha likes comic books; Keisha does not like comic books.
C Samantha likes comic books, and Keisha does not like comic books.
D Samantha and Keisha do and do not like comic books.

GO ON

Name ______________________ Date ______________

16 Which is the appositive phrase in the following sentence?

> The book, a mystery novel about a detective, is scary and exciting.

F The book,

G is scary and exciting.

H about a detective

J a mystery novel about a detective,

17 Which is an exclamatory sentence and should end with an exclamation point?

A Don't you just love reading on a rainy day

B I guess I'm just too busy to read

C Wow, that was a surprise ending

D Here, Julia, take this book home with you

18 Which is a declarative sentence and should end with a period?

F Which do you like better, *Anne of Green Gables or Dicey's Song*

G I think my favorite action book is *Hatchet* by Gary Paulsen

H Have you ever read one of Paulsen's books

J What an exciting story

Questions 19–20: A student wrote this paragraph about moving. It may need some changes or corrections. Read the paragraph. Then read each question. Fill in the circle of the correct answer on your answer document.

Moving Day

(1) The moving truck just rumbled up our driveway. (2) The movers are lugging all our furniture onto the front lawn. (3) I'm walking around the echoing rooms of my old house, trying to imagine what my new house will feel like. (4) I know it will be smaller; houses in the city are usually smaller than houses in the country. (5) It will be louder and more exciting with sirens blaring and car alarms beeping. (6) Where will we ride bikes in the city? (7) Now the movers are loading Samuel's bike into the truck. (8) Dad says there's a bike park just down the street from our new house. (9) Maybe I'll meet new friends there.

19 Which detail would be best to add just before sentence 9?

A I can go and check it out.

B My new school is bigger, too.

C I really hope the movers hurry.

D What will the family that bought our old house be like?

20 Which two sentences should be switched to organize the paragraph better?

F sentences 1 and 2

G sentences 3 and 4

H sentences 5 and 6

J sentences 6 and 7

GO ON

Name ______________________________ Date ______________

Part 2: Proofreading and Editing

Questions 21–30: Read the passages. Choose the best way to write each underlined part. Fill in the circle of the correct answer on your answer document.

Robots represent the <u>tecknology</u> (21) of the future. Already we use computerized robots to work in <u>factories!</u> (22) Within fifty years, <u>we will have using</u> (23) robots in our homes and work places. Robots may help many <u>people. Because</u> (24) in the future robots may be house cleaners, pet sitters, and cooks. In the working world, robots may someday be teachers! How would you like to learn from a robot? In <u>twenty-first century america</u> (25), robots will become quite common.

21 **A** technology
B tecnology
C tecknologie
D Make no change

22 **F** factories?
G factories,
H factories.
J Make no change

23 **A** we will be using
B we will have been used
C we have using
D Make no change

24 **F** people: because
G people? Because
H people because
J Make no change

25 **A** Twenty-first century America
B twenty-first century America
C Twenty-first century america
D Make no change

GO ON

Name ______________________ Date ______________

Dear Natalie:

I am having so much fun here in Florida! We get up early every day and go someplace exciting. Yesterday we went to a marine park and saw some amazing animals; dolphins (26), porpoises, manatees, penguins, and even a killer whale. I loved watching the dolphins jump. We sat in the front row for the hole show (27), and we got soaked! The penguins were really funny as they hobbled back and forth. Today we went to a nature center and explored (28) many of the exhibits. It was so cool! Tomorrow we'are going (29) to a theme park. I can't hardly wait (30) to ride the roller coaster!

I'll call you when we get home so I can show you all our pictures!

Your friend,

Amelia

26 **F** animals-dolphins
G animals, dolphins
H animals: dolphins
J Make no change

27 **A** an hole show
B the whole show
C the wholly show
D Make no change

28 **F** nature center and exploring
G nature center, explored
H nature center and we explored
J Make no change

29 **A** we're going
B wea're going
C were going
D Make no change

30 **F** cannot hardly wait
G can hardly wait
H can't hardly not wait
J Make no change

GO ON

Name ____ Date ____________________

Part 3: Writing — Expository

READ

Americans are fascinated by their pets. People read books and magazines and watch TV shows to learn everything they can about their pets.

THINK

Think about some of the things you need to know in order to take care of a pet. Do different pets require different kinds of knowledge, or are all pets basically the same when it comes to understanding how to care for them?

WRITE

Write an expository essay in which you explain what people need to know to take care of a pet.

As you write your composition, remember to —

- ☐ focus on a controlling idea that reflects what people need to know to take care of a pet
- ☐ organize your ideas logically and link them with transitions
- ☐ include appropriate facts and details to illustrate your points
- ☐ make sure your composition is no longer than one page

STOP

Name ______________________________ Date ______________

Progress Test 2

Part 1: Basic Elements of Writing

Questions 1–12: Read each sentence. Choose the best way to write the underlined part of the sentence. Fill in the circle of the correct answer on your answer document.

1 People have fear sharks since the beginning of history.

A have feared
B has been feared
C have fearing
D Make no change

2 The marine biologist is feeds the shark at the aquarium.

F fed
G feed
H feeding
J Make no change

3 There are many kinds of sharks, but only a few of them are dangerous to people.

A they
B theirs
C themselves
D Make no change

4 Eats and mated are the primary functions of sharks.

F Eating and mating
G Ate and mating
H Eating and mates
J Make no change

5 As the tiger shark swam toward our boat, I could see its fin along the surface of the water.

A above
B outside
C through
D Make no change

6 By 6:00 P.M. yesterday, we will have seen nine sharks.

F having seen
G have saw
H had seen
J Make no change

7 The aquarium is most busy on weekends.

A more busiest
B busiest
C most busiest
D Make no change

8 Because it was busy, we had to wait a long time to see the sharks.

F However
G Although
H Until
J Make no change

GO ON

Name ______________________________ Date ______________

9 Some sharks are herbivores, which eat only plants.

A eats
B eating
C eaten
D Make no change

10 A whale shark can grow to be more long than a school bus!

F longest
G longer
H more longer
J Make no change

11 Biology believe that some kinds of sharks are still undiscovered.

A Biologies
B Biologists'
C Biologists
D Make no change

12 Perhaps someday we will understand these remarkablest creatures better.

F remarkable
G remarkably
H remarkabler
J Make no change

Questions 13–18: Read each question and fill in the circle of the correct answer on your answer document.

13 How can this sentence best be expanded to include interesting details?

Hannah spins in dance class.

A Hannah really spins in her dance class.
B Hannah spins in her hip-hop dance class.
C Music flows through her body as Hannah spins around the room in dance class.
D Hannah spins in dance class and really likes to spin as she dances.

14 How can this sentence best be expanded to make it more interesting?

Justin jumps over the bump on his dirt bike.

F Pushing hard on the pedals and yanking back on the handlebars, Justin jumps over the three-foot bump on his dirt bike.
G Justin jumps and bumps on his dirt bike.
H Justin jumps on his broken, old, dirty dirt bike.
J Hearing the starter's gun, Justin races down the course, wanting to be the first to finish the race.

15 Which sentence contains an adverbial clause?

A Daniel washed the dishes until his hands were sore.
B Dad taught me how to fish last summer.
C Ryan is a great tennis player.
D Apples are full of essential vitamins and fiber.

GO ON

Name ______________________________ Date ______________

16 Which sentence contains consistent tenses?

F Because we win the game, we had pizza parties.

G Drink lots of water will help you digests your food better.

H Kai says that he believes personal robots are the future.

J Elephants are know to remember the tiniest detail.

17 Which sentence or sentences have correct pronoun-antecedent agreement?

A The game was tiring for Pete, which had the flu.

B If my computer breaks, I know how to fix it.

C Reece likes to eat, so they eats a lot of food.

D Both Luke and Anne like movies she can laugh with.

18 Which is the best way to improve this sentence to make it more interesting?

Ramon got home tired at noon.

F Ramon got home at noon and was tired.

G As the clock struck noon, Ramon staggered home exhausted.

H Ramon was tired and he got home exhausted at noon.

J At noon, Ramon, who was very tired, finally arrived at home.

Questions 19–20: A student wrote this paragraph. It may need some changes or corrections. Read the paragraph. Then read each question. Fill in the circle of the correct answer on your answer document.

Evacuation

(1) Huge waves thundered against the sea wall on our street. (2) The wind was blowing so hard that I barely heard my mom shout, (3) "The police said we have to evacuate!" (4) I grabbed my raincoat and my little brother's hand as we ran out the door. (5) Already the waves had risen over the sea wall and were crashing onto the street. (6) We drove slowly through the heavy rain to meet Dad at a restaurant near his office. (7) It seemed strange to be eating a quiet lunch while we watched the television for news of damage to our home.
(8) I had a cheeseburger with French fries. (9) It wasn't very good.
(10) We cheered when the newscaster finally said the storm had passed.

19 What type of paragraph is this?

A narrative

B persuasive

C response to a text

D expository

20 Which two sentences should be removed to improve this paragraph?

F sentences 1 and 2

G sentences 4 and 5

H sentences 6 and 7

J sentences 8 and 9

GO ON

Name ______________________________ Date ______________

Part 2: Proofreading and Editing

Questions 21–30: Read the passages. Choose the best way to write each underlined part. Fill in the circle of the correct answer on your answer document.

Recently, my family and me (21) went to see a movie at the theater. Mom said, "We haven't been to the theater in a while." (22) We had to travel more than an hour to the closest one but (23) it was well worth the trip! We all thought the movie was unbelieveable (24). There was a lot of action, and it was fun to watch it on the big screen. I hope we go to the theater again next weak (25).

21 **A** and, me
B and I
C and, I
D Make no change

22 **F** 'We haven't been to the theater in a while.'
G We haven't been to the theater in a while.
H (We haven't been to the theater in a while.)
J Make no change

23 **A** one; but
B one, but
C one: but
D Make no change

24 **F** unbeleavable
G unbelievible
H unbelievable
J Make no change

25 **A** week
B weake
C weeks
D Make no change

GO ON

Name ______________________________ Date ______________

May I have your attention please? As president of the <u>Orlando Fan club,</u> **26**

I am calling this meeting to order. We have a lot of work to do, so let's get

<u>started?</u> **27** At last week's <u>meeting the one at Nell's house we</u> **28** decided to make

"We Love Orlando" T-shirts. I have looked into the costs. Putting Orlando's

face on the shirt will cost five dollars extra for each shirt. Let's vote on <u>those.</u> **29**

How many of you think we should spend the extra money <u>to print</u> **30** Orlando's

face on the shirts?

26 **F** Orlando fan club
G Orlando Fan Club
H orlando fan club
J Make no change

27 **A** started,
B started!
C started.
D Make no change

28 **F** meeting . . . the one at Nell's house . . . we
G meeting-the one at Nell's house-we
H meeting—the one at Nell's house—we
J Make no change

29 **A** this
B them
C these
D Make no change

30 **F** and printing
G to prints
H and printed
J Make no change

GO ON

Name ______________________________ Date ______________

Part 3: Writing — Expository

READ

Some parts of our country are full of history. Everywhere you turn, you discover a historical place or the site of some significant or memorable event from the past.

THINK

Think of a historical place you have visited or seen on television. It could be a vacation spot or a place you go all the time. Think about what is historical about this place.

WRITE

Write an expository essay in which you explain why this place is historical.

As you write your composition, remember to —

- ☐ focus on a controlling idea that reflects a historical place you have visited
- ☐ organize your ideas logically and link them with transitions
- ☐ include appropriate facts and details to illustrate your points
- ☐ make sure your composition is no longer than one page

STOP

Name ______________________________ Date ______________

Post-test

Part 1: Basic Elements of Writing

Questions 1–12: Read each sentence. Choose the best way to write the underlined part of the sentence. Fill in the circle of the correct answer on your answer document.

1 Elvis Presley is called the "king" of rock and roll, <u>while</u> he did not invent it.

A as if
B therefore
C even though
D Make no change

2 Rock music <u>actual</u> draws from many other kinds of music.

F actualler
G actually
H actuals
J Make no change

3 Ragtime music, blues, and jazz <u>has</u> all contributed to rock music.

A have
B having
C to have
D Make no change

4 Today, rock artists even use <u>traditional</u> folk music to make their songs.

F tradition
G traditionally
H most traditional
J Make no change

5 Rock music has changed <u>alot</u> since Elvis sang his first song in the 1950s.

A allot
B a lots
C a lot
D Make no change

6 Hip-hop, funk, and rap all <u>was influenced</u> by rock music.

F is influencing
G were influenced
H was influencing
J Make no change

7 Both rap and techno music <u>is</u> characterized by a heavy beat.

A be
B was
C are
D Make no change

8 Many rock stars dance <u>across</u> the stage during their shows.

F outside
G within
H through
J Make no change

GO ON

Name ______________________________ Date ______________

9 He is one of the <u>famousest</u> rappers in the world.

A famously
B more famous
C most famous
D Make no change

10 Elijah and Olivia <u>listens</u> to music.

F listen
G listening
H listened
J Make no change

11 Oscar doesn't like <u>anyone</u> of those songs.

A much
B any
C neither
D Make no change

12 Rock music may have begun here, but the whole world loves <u>them.</u>

F they
G her
H it
J Make no change

Questions 13–18: Read each question and fill in the circle of the correct answer on your answer document.

13 Which is a complete sentence written correctly?

A The Old Man of the Mountain, as he was always known.
B Have you ever been to New Hampshire?
C Crumbling little by little each year until it fell.
D An incredibly life-like, natural rock formation.

14 Which is a run-on sentence and should be written as two sentences?

F People took steps to preserve the state landmark.
G They tried to stop the mountain face from crumbling.
H Using wires and netting, they tried to support the Old Man's face.
J Sadly they failed the Old Man of the Mountain crumbled.

15 Which is the subordinate clause in this sentence?

The game came to a close once Jordan scored the basket.

A The game came to a close
B came to a close
C once Jordan scored the basket
D scored the basket

GO ON

Name ______________________________ Date ______________

16 Which is the best way to combine these sentences to make a complex sentence?

We parked on the side of the road.
We looked up at the mountain peak.

F We parked on the side of the road; we looked up at the mountain peak.
G After we parked on the side of the road, we looked up at the mountain peak.
H We parked on the side of the road and we looked up at the mountain peak.
J We parked on the side of the road, or we looked up at the mountain peak.

17 Which is an interrogative sentence that should end with a question mark?

A I wonder if they will change the state symbol of New Hampshire
B What a shame to lose such an incredible landmark
C That would really be too bad
D What do you think about trying to rebuild the Old Man

18 Which is an imperative sentence that should end with a period?

F Look at this picture of the Old Man of the Mountain
G What incredible beauty
H Have you ever seen anything so remarkable
J I wonder if Denny remembers our trip to see the Old Man of the Mountain

Questions 19–20: A student wrote this paragraph about his favorite book. It may need some changes or corrections. Read the paragraph. Then read each question. Fill in the circle of the correct answer on your answer document.

A Thrilling Summer Read

(1) Are you looking for a great thriller? (2) Have summer reading lists got you down? (3) Well, don't fret because I have a great book for you! (4) I just finished reading *Caught in Time.* (5) It was action-packed and very exciting. (6) I couldn't turn the pages fast enough. (7) I just had to see what would happen next. (8) It is really scary; so if you like thrillers, this book is for you.

19 What type of paragraph is this?

A expository
B descriptive
C response to a text
D narrative

20 Which detail sentence would be best to add just before sentence 8?

F I stayed up all night reading.
G The book is very realistic and teaches a good lesson in the end.
H The beginning makes it seem like it's going to be a romance novel.
J Don't let that fool you!

GO ON

Name ______________________________ Date ______________

Part 2: Proofreading and Editing

Questions 21–30: Read the passages. Choose the best way to write each underlined part. Fill in the circle of the correct answer on your answer document.

Did you know that the sounds you hear during most movies are all recorded after the movie is <u>filmed!</u> (21) In order to take out distracting background noise, many movie directors use sound studios. <u>On these</u> (22) studios, the actors watch themselves on screen and speak their lines. <u>Trying</u> (23) to match their lip movements and <u>emoshuns</u> (24) exactly. Then sound makers tape important background noises to make the scenes sound <u>real;</u> (25) eventually all the taped sounds are combined to produce a soundtrack.

21 **A** filmed?
B filmed.
C filmed:
D Make no change

22 **F** Over these
G In these
H Beyond these
J Make no change

23 **A** Try
B Their trying
C They try
D Make no change

24 **F** emosions
G emotions
H emotins
J Make no change

25 **A** real,
B real:
C real—
D Make no change

GO ON

Name ________________________________ Date ________________

march fifteenth, 2011
26

Dear Pen Pal:

My names Ben Howard. I am a seventh grader and have studied
27

Spanish for two years. My favorite sport is soccer. When I'm not in school or playing soccer, I like to play video games. I play
28

'Island of Treasures' most often. What sports do you play? What do you do in
29

your free time?

Write back soon. I haven't never had a pen pal before.
30

Your new friend,

Ben Howard

26 F march 15
G March fifteen
H March 15
J Make no change

27 A names'
B name's
C name'is
D Make no change

28 F soccer; I
G soccer-I
H soccer: I
J Make no change

29 A *Island of Treasures*
B "Island of Treasures"
C Island of Treasures
D Make no change

30 F had never haven't
G have never had
H have not never had
J Make no change

GO ON

Name ______________________ Date ______________

Part 3: Writing — Narrative

READ

Many things we do can make us feel proud. We can help someone, teach someone something new, solve a problem, or fix something that's broken. There are countless examples of things that can give us a sense of pride.

THINK

Think about something you have done recently that made you feel proud. What did you do? Why did it give you a feeling of pride?

WRITE

Write a narrative essay describing what you did that made you feel proud.

As you write your composition, remember to —

- ☐ focus on a controlling idea that reflects something you did that made you feel proud
- ☐ organize your ideas logically and link them with transitions
- ☐ include appropriate facts and details about the event and communicate its importance
- ☐ make sure your composition is no longer than one page

STOP